NOT-FOR-PARENTS

HOW TO BE A

DINOSAUR HUNTER

your globe-trotting, time-traveling guide

By Scott Forbes

Illustrations by
James Gulliver Hancock

lonely planet

CONTENTS

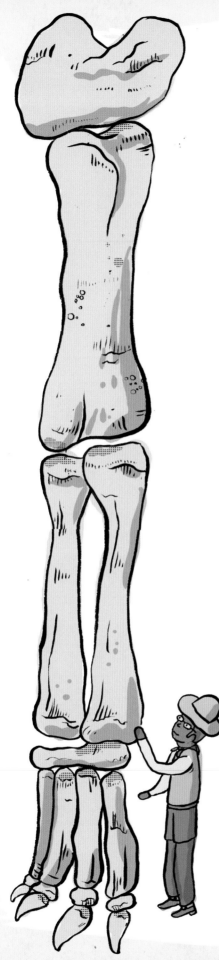

BURIED TREASURE

You've been in the field for weeks. You're dirty, wet, and finding virtually nothing. But suddenly, as you brush at a dusty mound, a smooth, round shape emerges. You realize that it's the bulging joint of a massive leg bone almost as big as you—part of a colossal dinosaur that died at this spot roughly 120 million years ago. It's exactly what you were looking for. And it could be the find of the century!

More dinosaurs!

Watch out! You never know what a rockfall might reveal. See page 18.

Check that you have all the tools you need on page 9.

Possible coprolite? Is that good? Find out on page 17.

HUNTER'S QUEST

Your quest is to assemble the world's greatest collection of dinosaur fossils. To do that you'll need to search the world and travel back in time to learn more about what dinosaurs looked like and how they lived. This book will show you how to do both.

Globe-trotting

Dinosaur fossils have been unearthed all over the world, but some places have provided particularly rich pickings. The following pages will show you the world's richest fossil sites and tell you about the treasures uncovered there and the people who found them. What else awaits *your* discovery?

Time traveling

Firsthand experience of the dinosaur world will help you understand your finds and bring them back to life. So you'll also whiz back to the age of the dinosaurs, the Mesozoic Era, which lasted from 250 million years ago to 65 million years ago and spanned three periods: the Triassic, Jurassic, and Cretaceous.

PSST!
WHAT DO YOU CALL A DINOSAUR WITH ONE EYE?
DYATHINKHESAURUS!

Dressing for success

COOL, HUH?

You'll need to dress and pack for all kinds of terrain and weather conditions. Forget fashion statements and leave your party gear at home—you'll need practical, durable clothing that you don't mind messing up while digging around in the dirt: tough boots for tramping through rocky terrain; a broad-brimmed hat for long hours in the sometimes scorching Sun; and warm, waterproof clothing for when the weather turns stormy.

Tools of the trade

A typical dinosaur hunter's kit includes the following trusty items:

Rock hammer and chisels for chipping at hard surfaces

Goggles to protect eyes from flying splinters

Hard hat if working in quarries or at cliffs

Binoculars and magnifying glass

First-aid kit

Shovel and trowel for digging

Brushes for dusting off

Picks and probes for prodding, scratching, and scraping

Boxes and tissue paper for wrapping and storing small treasures

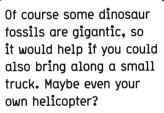

Of course some dinosaur fossils are gigantic, so it would help if you could also bring along a small truck. Maybe even your own helicopter?

SPOT THE DINOSAUR?

You know what you're looking for, don't you? Dinosaurs, of course! And you know what they look like, right? Lizard-like? Yep, but so were many other creatures. Big? Some as huge as houses, but others no higher than your knee. Scary? Heart-stoppingly terrifying in many cases, but some were small, harmless, fluffy, and even, well, kind of cute.

Amphicoelias

Little and large

Microceratops

Though you might have a typical dinosaur in mind, you'll find that they came in all shapes and sizes. As its name suggests, *Microceratops* was a tiny guy, standing just 2 ft. (60 cm) tall. It would barely reach your waist and only the ankles of *Amphicoelias*, one of the biggest dinosaurs yet discovered. It may have been up to 200 ft. (60 m) long and weighed 132 tons (120 tonnes)—as much as 24 elephants!

Many prehistoric creatures are referred to as dinosaurs but were not actually dinosaurs at all. Can you spot the real dinosaur in this reptilian lineup?

Odd one out?

ER, TWEET, TWEET?

1 **2** **3** **4**

DIMETRODON
That spiny sail, those alarming teeth . . . surely? But no. *Dimetrodon* lived 40 million years before the first dinosaurs and was more closely related to mammals.

PTERANODON
Those wings are kind of a giveaway, aren't they? Though often referred to as "flying dinosaurs," the so-called pterosaurs were actually a separate group of reptiles.

POSTOSUCHUS
With its upright stance, small arms, and scary jaws, *Postosuchus* is a dead ringer for *Tyrannosaurus*. But it is part of another reptile group, the rauisuchians.

CITIPATI
Feathers? Stumpy wings? A beaklike mouth? This has to be some kind of prehistoric parrot! No. *Citipati* was a birdlike dinosaur of the Late Cretaceous period.

Genuine article?

So what distinguishes a dinosaur from other prehistoric reptiles? We'd better get that straight before you head off. Among other minor differences, dinosaurs had particularly long snout bones called vomers. And they had a long crest or ridge on the upper arm bone. But what set them apart more than anything else was that their hip bones allowed them to stand and walk upright—unlike other reptiles.

THEY DON'T STAND A CHANCE!

100% DINO

A lizard has legs that splay out to the sides. This keeps it low to the ground and causes its body to sway as it walks. In turn that makes it hard to breathe—and makes running exhausting!

Like some other reptiles of the prehistoric past and present, a crocodile has more upright hind legs. This allows it to run on only its back legs for short distances. Still pretty tiring, though.

A dinosaur's back legs had a right-angled joint so that its leg bones pointed downward. This made standing, breathing, and running easier—and gave it a head start against its rivals.

Hip, hip!

Dinosaurs eventually evolved into various groups or families, but starting early on they were divided into two main groups according to the shape of their hip bones: the "lizard-hipped" saurischians and the "bird-hipped" ornithischians. The saurischians included all meat eaters (carnivores) and some plant eaters (herbivores), but the ornithischians were all plant eaters.

In saurischians such as Tyrannosaurus, the bone between the hips, called the pubic bone or pubis, points forward.

Tyrannosaurus

Pubis

Edmontosaurus

Pubis

In ornithischians, such as the giant plant eater, Edmontosaurus, the larger section of the pubis points backward.

TIME OF THEIR LIVES

Dinosaurs appeared about 238 million years ago and pretty much ruled the world for 160 million years. That's a heck of a lot longer than humans have been around. Yet in terms of the truly epic history of our planet, it was just another passing phase.

Earth span

Okay, on your feet! Arms stretched out! Imagine that the span of your arms is the history of our planet. Geologists divide that history into four eras. The first, the Precambrian, starts with the formation of Earth 4.6 billion years ago—at the tip of your right hand—and ends 542 million years ago—at your left wrist. The second, the Paleozoic, ends 250 million years ago—at the top of your palm. The age of the dinosaurs, the Mesozoic Era, starts at the bottom

Earth forms

Age of the dinosaurs

Human era

of your middle finger and ends, 65 million years ago, at the top joint, where the last era, the Cenozoic, starts. Humans have been around for just 200,000 years. Our entire history takes place on that fingertip.

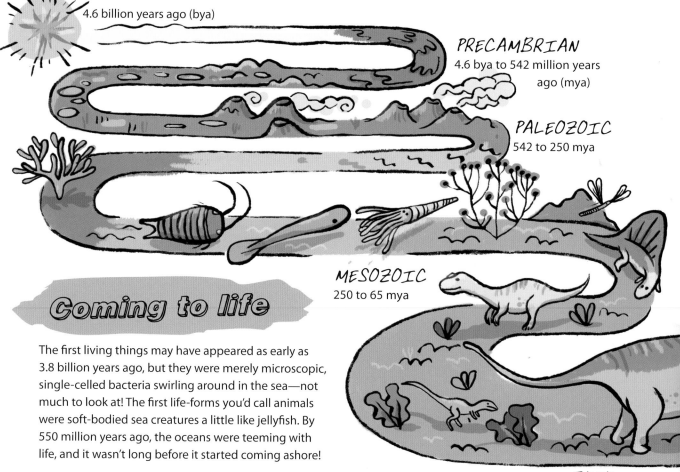

4.6 billion years ago (bya)

PRECAMBRIAN
4.6 bya to 542 million years ago (mya)

PALEOZOIC
542 to 250 mya

MESOZOIC
250 to 65 mya

Triassic
250 to 208 mya

Coming to life

The first living things may have appeared as early as 3.8 billion years ago, but they were merely microscopic, single-celled bacteria swirling around in the sea—not much to look at! The first life-forms you'd call animals were soft-bodied sea creatures a little like jellyfish. By 550 million years ago, the oceans were teeming with life, and it wasn't long before it started coming ashore!

Catch the drift?

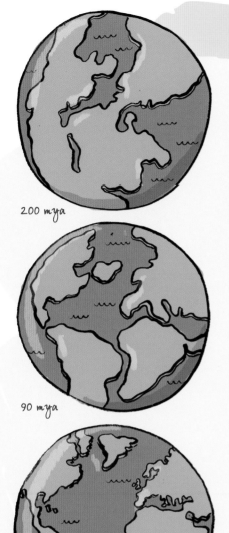

200 mya

90 mya

Today

Because of heat rising from Earth's hot core, our planet's crust and landmasses are always on the move—though very, very slowly. When dinosaurs first emerged, all of the continents were joined together in one "supercontinent" called Pangaea. Since then, they have gradually broken up and drifted apart to form the shapes that we recognize today.

AHA! I THINK I'M GETTING THE PICTURE!

PUZZLE PIECES

Look at a world map and you'll see that South America and Africa could fit neatly together, like two pieces of a jigsaw puzzle. Other continents could also fit together. Can you spot them? German meteorologist Alfred Wegener noticed this in the early 1900s and by 1912 had proposed the now accepted theory of "continental drift."

The continents move at about the rate your fingernails grow.

DINOSAURS RULE!

CENOZOIC
65 mya to present

Jurassic
208 to 144 mya

Cretaceous
144 to 65 mya

Tertiary
65 to 2 mya

Quaternary
2 mya to present

WHERE'D THEY GO?

If dinosaurs ruled the world for 160 million years, how come there are none around now? What happened?! Well, the reasons are still hotly debated, but one thing's for sure: all dinosaurs suddenly vanished 65 million years ago—or almost all . . .

Weather woes

> DO YOU SMELL SMOKE?

Some scientists think the so-called Cretaceous mass extinction might have been caused by climate change—it got so hot or so cold that the dinosaurs couldn't survive. Others say that there were major volcanic eruptions and these not only covered huge areas of Earth with lava but also blocked out the Sun with their ash and spread poisonous gases all over the planet. Either way: *not* a good time to be around.

One strike and out

> UH-OH!

The most likely theory is that a huge meteorite struck Earth, setting half the world on fire, unleashing tsunamis, filling the air with smoke, blocking out the Sun, and creating acid rain that killed most plants. And, in fact, a giant meteorite did hit Earth around 66 million years ago, leaving a gigantic crater now buried beneath the southeast coast of Mexico.

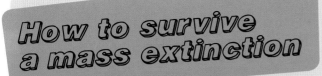

How to survive a mass extinction

Dinosaurs weren't the only ones to disappear. In fact, about 85 percent of living things vanished. Yet some crafty critters survived, including birds, insects and—lucky for you—mammals. How did they do it? How do you beat mass extinction?

Stay small. Little creatures need less food, so they can survive when food is scarce. And they can hide out in even the tightest spots.

Live underground or under water. That should protect you from blasts, fire, poisonous gases—whatever's going on "up there."

Wear protection. A hard case or shell, especially one that you can retreat inside, might just get you through some bumpy times.

Be adaptable. Don't be picky about where you live. Learn to cope with forests, deserts—whatever! Disaster strikes? Move on!

Eat a varied diet. Picky eaters have had it! A taste for everything will help you deal with that minimal postextinction menu.

Be lucky! Try to be in the right place at the right time: far from the trouble spots and, ideally, just snoozing through it all!

> DID I MISS SOMETHING?

Dinosaur descendants

Dinosaurs died out, but a few of their relatives survived. Which of the following is the closest relative of the dinosaurs?

Lizard

Crocodile

Dog

Bird

Think lizard? Think again! The answer is the bird. Dogs are no relation. Lizards evolved from a separate group of reptiles. Crocodiles belong to the ancient group of reptiles from which dinosaurs evolved, the archosaurs, and are therefore distant cousins. But birds evolved directly from dinosaurs. So you may have several dinosaurs in your backyard. Right now.

> Surprisingly, birds didn't evolve from bird-hipped dinosaurs but from lizard-hipped ones.

WHAT'S LEFT?

Birds aside, dinosaurs didn't survive the Cretaceous mass extinction, nor did they disappear completely. Their remains lie all over the world. We call most of these remains fossils—and fossils are what you are looking for.

Lasting impressions

A fossil is a relic of a creature that lived in prehistoric times. Most dinosaur fossils are bones or teeth that have turned to stone underground, long after their owners breathed their last and were buried by shifting sands or soil. Other fossils take the form of imprints left in rock layers by bones, skin, feathers, or even whole animals.

No dinosaur ever thought about becoming a fossil, of course. But if you were to aim for future fossil preservation, this would be the best strategy.

How to become a fossil

Die on soft mud or sand. It's particularly good for preserving bodies, and the fine particles make for more detailed imprints.

Perish near—or, even better, in—a river or lake. Water will slowly deposit sediments on top of your body without disturbing its position. Slow and steady!

I HOPE SOMEONE FINDS ME SOON!

Die where Earth's plates don't move much. Some rocks get squeezed and twisted by plate movements, which can make a real mess of your remains. If the rocks are little disturbed, your bones will have time to be replaced by minerals and turn to stone.

Keep your fingers crossed that, at some point in the far future, landslides, erosion, or helpful dinosaur hunters reveal your magnificent bones to the world. Then you might even make it to a museum display—and lasting fame!

Permanent prints

In some places, dinosaur tracks in soft mud have hardened over millions of years, leaving footprints in solid rock. These track marks can tell you a great deal about the type, size, walking motion, and even the speed of the dinosaurs that made them.

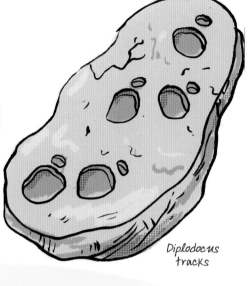

Tyrannosaurus tracks

Diplodocus tracks

EGGS-ACTLY WHAT YOU'RE LOOKING FOR!

Fossilized eggs have been unearthed in many parts of the world—some still containing fossilized baby animals! From these you can learn how dinosaurs grew and cared for their young.

AREN'T THEY GREAT?

Prehistoric poop

Found a round, hard fossil? It could be a piece of dinosaur poop, or coprolite. No, don't say, "Yuck!" and fling it away. It could tell you what that dinosaur ate, how it digested food—even how big its bottom was. Many museums have impressive displays of dinosaur droppings!

DIGGING AROUND

Fossils lie hidden in many places. They're in rocks, under sand, below the ocean—maybe even beneath your feet right now. But where are the best places to look, and how do you figure out where to start digging?

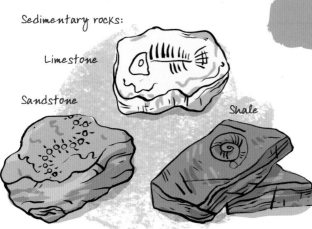

Sedimentary rocks:

Limestone

Sandstone

Shale

It's sedimentary!

There are three types of rocks: igneous, metamorphic, and sedimentary. Igneous rocks formed from molten rock. Metamorphic rocks are rocks that have been squeezed by titanic forces inside Earth's crust. There's not much chance of fossils surviving inside either of those! Sedimentary rocks, however, formed when tiny grains of stone were slowly laid down (often underwater) and then cemented together to form rock. Undisturbed sedimentary rock is the type of rock most likely to contain fossils—so seek it out.

Coming to light

Apart from being found by deliberate searching and digging, fossils may be revealed by chance as a result of natural processes or human activities.

Rivers cut deep into rock layers, often exposing fossils.

Landslides sometimes conveniently rearrange the scenery.

Carving through hillsides to create roadways can open a window onto past events.

Digging deep underground to create tunnels might lead to discoveries of dinosaur remains.

How to find a fossil

Professional fossil hunters might use high-tech instruments to help locate the right types of rocks. But after that finding fossils comes down to skillful use of a pair of tools we all have—our eyes.

Roadcuts are a great place to study rock layers—but watch out for traffic!

1 Find an area of exposed, crumbly rock layers, such as a riverbed, cliff, or roadcut. Walk slowly along the rock face and scan the ground for possible bone fragments.

2 If you find a bone fragment, try to figure out where it might have come from. If you are on a riverbed, for example, follow the watercourse upstream to the possible source.

3 Look for larger bones protruding from rocks. Study any finds carefully to figure out how large they might be and how easily they can be extracted.

4 Find out from your local museum or government whether you can dig there. Turn to page 144 and start planning your excavation.

DIG DEEPER

• • • • • • • • • • • • • • • • • • • •

LOCAL MUSEUMS

One of the best ways to find out about the rocks in your area, as well as dinosaur remains, is to visit your local museum. You might even find a friendly dinosaur expert, or paleontologist, who can direct you to local fossil sites. Some museums even organize dinosaur digs that you can join.

She found sea shells—and much, much more—on the seashore. See page 30.

Big bottom? Elephant leg bone? What could it be? See page 24.

Who dined inside a dino? Find out on page 27.

Europe's biggest? Check it out on page 38.

The first dinosaur egg was found in France. See page 35.

ENGLAND

LONDON •
Dorset ✕   •Dover
     • Isle of Wight   ✕ • BRUSSELS
                              Bernissart

GERMANY

• PARIS

Solnhofen ✕
MUNICH •

FRANCE

SPAIN

✕
Teruel

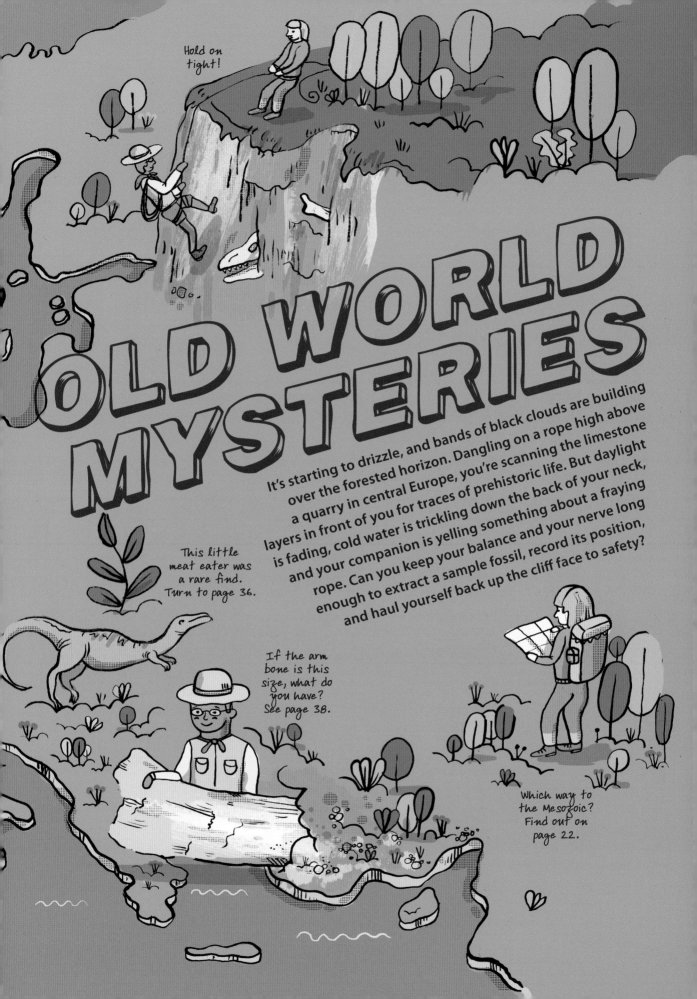

Hold on tight!

OLD WORLD MYSTERIES

It's starting to drizzle, and bands of black clouds are building over the forested horizon. Dangling on a rope high above a quarry in central Europe, you're scanning the limestone layers in front of you for traces of prehistoric life. But daylight is fading, cold water is trickling down the back of your neck, and your companion is yelling something about a fraying rope. Can you keep your balance and your nerve long enough to extract a sample fossil, record its position, and haul yourself back up the cliff face to safety?

This little meat eater was a rare find. Turn to page 36.

If the arm bone is this size, what do you have? See page 38.

Which way to the Mesozoic? Find out on page 22.

HUNTER'S QUEST

Europe is where dinosaur hunting took off. It's where the first dinosaur fossils were found and where it was decided that dinosaurs would be called, well, "dinosaurs." So it's a great place to start! Make sure you visit its magnificent museums to learn about early discoveries and view some prize skeletons before heading out into the field.

Going underground?

Most of Europe's best fossil sites are in the western part of the continent, especially in southern England, northern France, and southern Germany, where Mesozoic rocks lie close to the surface. There's plenty of transportation in these areas, so getting to sites is a cinch. But the fact that this is one of the most densely populated parts of the world can present other challenges!

SEE WHAT I REALLY LOOKED LIKE ON PAGE 47.

Plateosaurus

Triassic target

Europe is rich in fossils from the late Jurassic and Cretaceous, so it's a good place to stock up on specimens from those periods. Earlier finds are rarer, though one Triassic dinosaur that has been found all over western Europe is *Plateosaurus*, a long-necked plant eater. Can you find one to add to your collection?

Plateosaurus has been found at more than 50 sites in Germany.

Hanging around

Away from cities and crowds, good places to look for fossils include ocean cliffs, quarries, and mountains. Exploring areas such as these requires extra care and definitely a hard hat or helmet to guard against rockfalls. You might even need to be prepared to do some tricky climbing or rappelling. Hope you have a head for heights!

EASTERN PROMISE

If you want to make a name for yourself, you might head to eastern Europe. Few fossils have been found there, but wide bands of Mesozoic rocks run through western Russia, so it could just be that very few people have made the effort to look! Skip winter, though, unless you're a glutton for punishment.

THERE BE MONSTERS!

When people first started digging up giant bones, they came up with all sorts of theories to explain them. Some thought that they were the remains of dragons still hiding out in remote parts of the world. Others believed that they might be the bones of giant humans that once roamed Earth.

The plot thickens

In 1677 English naturalist Robert Plot provided the first written description of what is now known to have been a dinosaur bone. It was the bottom part of a thigh bone of a *Megalosaurus*. Not that Plot realized that. He proclaimed that it was "the Bone of some elephant, brought hither [to England] by the Romans." Others thought that it must be part of a giant human from long ago.

NOT MUCH MEAT LEFT ON THAT.

Gone but no longer forgotten

By the early 1800s scientists had realized that some creatures from the distant past were no longer around. When Oxford, England, naturalist William Buckland found a large jawbone, he decided that it came from an extinct giant lizard. In 1824 he wrote an article about the lizard (the first description ever of a dinosaur) and named it *Megalosaurus*, which means—yes, you guessed it!—"giant lizard." Buckland was an eccentric character who kept dozens of animals in his house, including a bear that he dressed in a scholar's cap and gown.

Buckland liked to eat a piece of every animal he studied, so guests never knew what might be on the menu! Baked guinea pig, anyone?

NO WONDER THOSE ROMANS WERE SO SUCCESSFUL!

DENTAL RECORDS

In 1822 English doctor Gideon Mantell pulled some large fossilized teeth from a quarry in Sussex, England. A couple of years later he realized they were similar to those of an iguana, so he named the ancient, extinct creature they had come from *Iguanodon*, meaning "iguana tooth."

HORN OF A DILEMMA

In the 1830s Mantell was given a large block of fossilized bones from another *Iguanodon*, including an unusual fossil with a sharp point. Uncertain what it was, he illustrated it as a horn in one of his sketches. Much later it was realized that the "horn" was actually one of the *Iguanodon*'s thumb claws. Oops!

THAT GETS THE THUMBS DOWN FROM ME!

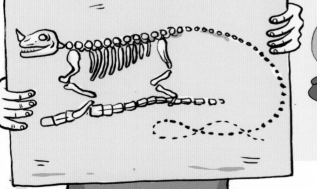

The large block of fossilized *Iguanodon* bones became famous as the "Mantell-piece"!

DINO-MANIA!

LET'S SEE, "SCARY SLITHERERS OR RASCALLY REPTILES?" HMM . . .

With more and more fossils of giant reptiles coming to light, scientists began to think of these ancient animals as a separate group of extinct creatures. And in 1842 English anatomist Richard Owen decided to call them *Dinosauria*, meaning "terrible lizards." It wasn't a very accurate name, as it turned out, but it sure caught on!

Truly terrible?

Owen was an expert in animal anatomy—he liked nothing better than dissecting a dead creature or two from London Zoo. And he correctly spotted that his "terrible lizards" had different hips from other reptiles—ones that allowed them to walk upright. But of course, as you now know, dinosaurs weren't always terrible and they weren't lizards at all, but a different kind of reptile.

THE LATEST THING

Nevertheless, the public was thrilled by Owen's writings, lectures, and outlandish publicity stunts. In the early 1850s Owen and sculptor Benjamin Waterhouse Hawkins built life-size models of huge dinosaurs to be displayed on the grounds of the Crystal Palace, a spectacular glass pavilion in London, England. When the park opened, 40,000 people rushed to view these "terrible" re-creations. Visitors could even buy souvenir mini models to terrify their friends!

Many of Hawkins's dinosaurs are still on display in Crystal Palace Park.

How to make a dinosaur

Hawkins's sculptures took some building. Each one contained 30 tons (27 tonnes) of clay. His *Iguanodon* model alone required 600 bricks, more than 7,000 tiles, 38 casks of cement, and 90 casks of broken stone. How would you do it?

6 Tile and paint model.

EASY, HUH?

1 Draw the dinosaur.

2 Make a small model.

5 Cast a concrete model using the mold and place on top of iron frame and brick foundations.

3 Build a life-size clay statue.

4 Make a mold of the statue.

LUCKY FOR YOU ALL I'M A HERBIVORE!

THANK GOODNESS THEY'RE EXTINCT!

DINNER ON ME!

To celebrate the opening of the park, Owen held a special event on New Year's Eve in 1853. He invited a group of leading scientists to dine with him—inside Hawkins's partially completed model of an *Iguanodon*!

DIG DEEPER

NATURAL HISTORY MUSEUM

Being the birthplace of dinosaur hunting, Europe has some of the finest fossil collections in the world. And one of the best is on display at the Natural History Museum in London, England, which was established by none other than Richard Owen. It's a must-see for every dinosaur hunter!

CLOSED DOORS

In the mid-1800s museums were thought of as centers of research and were essentially closed to the public. Anyone who wanted to go to the British Museum, for example, had to apply in writing, prove they were a real scientist, and pass an interview. Most fossils were kept hidden in cabinets. Owen changed all that. He encouraged the public to visit, put many specimens on display, and even attached labels to explain what they were. Helpful!

GOSH, I THOUGHT IT WAS A RAILROAD STATION.

Today the Natural History Museum has about 9 million fossils in its collection.

GET ME ONE OF THOSE NOW!

THE FAINTEST CLUE

Passing through Paris? If so, don't miss its Natural History Museum, which has 2.7 million items in its paleontology collection. Learn to recognize local fossils by checking out French finds such as *Plateosaurus*, *Compsognathus*, and *Variraptor*. Much of the collection was assembled by France's pioneer paleontologist, Georges Cuvier. As early as 1808 he suggested that long-extinct reptiles had once ruled the world.

Cuvier could identify some prehistoric creatures from a single tooth. Now that's a useful skill!

TALL, DARK, SCALY, LIKES TO EAT PLANTS . . .

ALL THE RAGE

Wealthy donors made their own giant contributions. In 1905, in response to a request from Great Britain's King Edward VII, Scottish-born US millionaire Andrew Carnegie gave the museum a complete *Diplodocus* skeleton. Soon everyone wanted one—and Carnegie was happy to oblige. He had copies made for heads of state in France, Germany, Austria, Italy, Spain, Russia, Argentina, and Mexico.

COOL! I'VE GOT TO HAVE ONE TOO!

DOWN ON THE DOWNS

Just below the surface of southern England lie bands of Triassic, Jurassic, and Cretaceous rocks. Much is now covered by roads and buildings, but if you leave the hustle and bustle of the towns and head south to the quieter coastal countryside known as the downlands, or downs, you'll find treasures aplenty.

White Cliffs of Dover

Coastal clusters

Jurassic rocks reach the coast in Dorset in southwestern England, while much of England's southeast (where Gideon Mantell found his *Iguanodon* fossils) is Cretaceous territory, including the famous White Cliffs of Dover. These chalk, or limestone, formations are an especially good spot for finding fossils of prehistoric sea creatures.

Mary Anning's activities are said to have inspired the tongue twister "She sells seashells on the seashore."

BY THE SEASIDE

In 1811, at the age of just twelve, a young Dorset girl, Mary Anning made an astounding discovery while looking for fossils on the seashore with her father: a complete fossil of an ichthyosaur, a sea-dwelling reptile of the Jurassic period. That was the start of Mary's amazing career as a fossil hunter. She found many more important fossils, including other marine reptiles as well as pterosaurs (flying reptiles) and shellfish, some of which she sold to major museums. And she became highly skilled at extracting fossils from rocks without damaging them.

ARMOR PLATED

One of the first complete dinosaur fossils—and the first armored dinosaur to be discovered—was dug up in Dorset, England, and named by Richard Owen in 1859. A Jurassic herbivore about 10 ft. (3 m) long, *Scelidosaurus* was covered in bony plates and had rows of spikes on its neck and limbs.

Other dinosaurs to search for here include *Thecodontosaurus*, *Cetiosaurus*, and *Echinodon*.

THUMBS UP!

How would you feel if you came across this colossal claw? Happy its owner's not still around? Amateur dinosaur hunter William Walker struck it lucky in 1983 when he cut the claw out of a clay pit in Surrey, England. Experts followed up on his find and soon found an entire skeleton. They called it *Baryonyx*, meaning "heavy claw."

Baryonyx was a fish eater and used its deadly claw to skewer prey.

TREASURE ISLAND

It's only 23 mi. (37 km) wide and 13 mi. (20 km) from top to bottom, but the Isle of Wight, just off England's south coast, is the BIG place in Europe for dinosaur hunting. Hundreds of fossils have been found on the island, from more than 20 different species.

A helping hand

Dinosaur hunters get a helping hand from nature here, as ocean, wind, and rain often batter the island's coast, gouging at rocks and exposing new fossils. So a good time to go hunting is after a big storm, and the best places to check out are the southeast and southwest coasts. But be careful on the rocks, and watch out for big waves and incoming tides!

Hypsilophodon

Sticking together

You'll have a good chance of finding fossils of a small, beaked, plant-eating dinosaur called *Hypsilophodon*. Hundreds of these have been found, often in groups, which suggests that they lived in herds—and died together, possibly in flash floods.

Neovenator

Watch out!

Small dinosaurs such as *Hypsilophodon* would have been constantly keeping watch for rampaging predators such as *Neovenator*, a terrifying flesh eater measuring 25 ft. (7.5 m) in length and armed with rows of razor-sharp teeth and long, hooked claws. *Neovenator* was first found on the Isle of Wight, in 1978, and was given its name—"new hunter"—in 1996.

In 2009 five-year-old Daisy Morris found the bones of a pterosaur on the island. It turned out to be a new species and in 2013 was named, in her honor, *Vectidraco daisymorrisae*.

Down on the farm

Imagine finding a giant dinosaur in your backyard. That's more or less what happened in 1992 to the Phillips family, owners of a farm near Brighstone on the southwest coast of the Isle of Wight. Paleontologists dug up part of the skeleton of a brachiosaur on their land. This huge plant eater may have been 50 ft. (15 m) long. Bones of an even bigger brachiosaur—possibly more than 66 ft. (20 m) long—were found on the island in 2004.

I DON'T REMEMBER PLANTING THOSE.

DIG DEEPER

. . . .

DINOSAUR ISLE

There aren't many places where you can look at fossils inside a model of a giant flying reptile. Dinosaur Isle, the Isle of Wight's major museum, was designed in the shape of an enormous pterosaur and houses a fantastic collection of more than 1,000 local finds. On display are *Megalosaurus* and *Iguanodon* skeletons and a life-size replica of *Polacanthus*, a spiky armored dinosaur discovered in 1865. You can also sign up here for fossil hunts and digs.

LONG LOST COUSIN

Another alarming island resident, dug up in 1997, was *Eotyrannus*, a smaller, slimmer ancestor of *Tyrannosaurus*.

DINO MINE

Across the English Channel, dinosaur fossil sites are scattered across central France. There are fewer places to dig farther north in the low-lying lands of the Netherlands and Belgium, yet, even here, you never know what might lie far beneath your feet!

Chance find

WHAT ON EARTH WERE THEY DOING DOWN HERE?!

In 1878, while tunneling 980 ft. (300 m) underground near the Belgian town of Bernissart, a team of coal miners came across a cluster of what at first appeared to be old tree trunks. Instead, they proved to be the bones of dozens of *Iguanodons*.

Brussels sprouts a hero

More than 140 tons (130 tonnes) of bones were dug out by the miners and sent to Belgium's Natural History Museum in Brussels. There a fossil expert named Louis Dollo faced the daunting task of sorting them into some kind of order. Where would you start?! Heroically, over several years, Dollo built 30 *Iguanodon* skeletons, some of them complete.

Dollo displayed *Iguanodon* walking on two feet, but experts now think it usually walked on four.

DIG DEEPER

• •

BELGIAN MUSEUM OF NATURAL SCIENCES

It might have changed its name, but most other things at Brussels's former Natural History Museum have stayed the same, including Louis Dollo's *Iguanodon* skeletons. Make the trip and you can still see all 30—part of the largest dinosaur display in Europe!

CLIMB EVERY MOUNTAIN

THAT COULD MAKE A BIG OMELET!

NOW, LET'S SEE. "THE HIP BONE'S CONNECTED TO THE LEG BONE . . ."

In France it could pay to head for high ground. The Alps and Pyrenees mountain ranges have both yielded fascinating fossils. The footprints of giant plant-eating dinosaurs have been found on Alpine slopes, including, in 2009 near Lyon, France, some of the biggest ever found—up to 6 ft. (2 m) across. In 1859 a priest living in the Pyrenees, Jean-Jacques Pouech, made the first discovery ever of dinosaur eggs. Noting that they were four times the size of ostrich eggs, Pouech decided they had been laid by giant birds. But paleontologists later proved they were dinosaur eggs.

A BIRD IN THE HAND

Some of the world's most valuable fossils are ones that show the link between dinosaurs and birds. They're a must-have for your collection! The first fossil birds, as they are known, came from southern Germany, where you might still come across these and other prehistoric rarities.

FINE FEATHERED

Head for the little village of Solnhofen near Munich, Germany. It sits on a wide expanse of fine-grained late Jurassic limestone, which has preserved many fossils in amazing detail, and the countryside is dotted with quarries where you can try your luck. In 1859 quarry workers unearthed the skeleton of what appeared to be a small dinosaur with wings and feathers. It was named *Archaeopteryx*, meaning "ancient wing," and later sold to Richard Owen at the British Museum in London.

Ready for takeoff

Ten other *Archaeopteryx* skeletons have since been found around Solnhofen. Although *Archaeopteryx* was a small, meat-eating dinosaur, it is also thought of as the first bird because its wings and feathers helped it glide or fly short distances while pursuing prey.

THAT WOULD NEVER FIT IN MY CANARY'S CAGE!

LAST MEAL

Around the same time as *Archaeopteryx* was found, the quarries of Solnhofen coughed up another curiosity: the skeleton of a small, two-legged, carnivorous dinosaur, *Compsognathus*. It was the first fossil to show that dinosaur predators didn't have to be enormous—*Compsognathus* was the size of a little dog but had rows of viciously sharp teeth and could move at high speed. Amazingly, the remains of its last meal were visible in the fossil: an unlucky lizard.

Starfish

Ichthyosaur

Archaeopteryx

High and dry

Eager to stock up on marine fossils? You're in the right place for that too. Beautifully preserved skeletons of prehistoric sea-dwelling reptiles, crocodilians, and fish have surfaced at Solnhofen as well as at nearby Holzmaden. So detailed are the Holzmaden finds that in fossils of dolphin-like ichthyosaurs you can see every bone and fin and even babies inside pregnant females.

Only one other *Compsognathus* skeleton has been found, in France in 1971.

Compsognathus fossil from Solnhofen

Compsognathus

ROCKIN' OUT

The eastern interior of Spain is a high, dry place with expanses of rocky ground. Only in recent years have paleontologists realized that the boulders and stones that litter this landscape conceal countless Cretaceous fossils—including some of the biggest dinosaur bones ever found.

Scaling up

If you're looking at an upper arm bone, or humerus, 6 ft. (178 cm) long, you've got one colossal creature on your hands! That's what Spanish paleontologists realized after finding such a bone in Riodeva near the town of Teruel in 2004. They named their new find *Turiasaurus riodevensis* and figured out that it was a long-necked plant eater, or sauropod, that roamed the area 150 million years ago.

I'M HUGE IN EUROPE, YOU KNOW!

In 2012 paleontologists painstakingly pieced together tiny bone fragments to reconstruct the skull of Turiasaurus.

It's a whopper!

In 2010 a 6-ft. (2-m)-long femur, or thighbone, from the same species was found. It confirmed estimates that *Turiasaurus* was more than 100 ft. (30 m) from head to tail and weighed a whopping 44 tons (40 tonnes). That made it the biggest dinosaur ever found in Europe!

Humerus

Be prepared: Spain's Teruel district is notorious for its harsh climate—baking hot in the summer and freezing cold in the winter.

BUMPER BOUNTY

The remains of hundreds of other giant plant eaters, known as titanosaurs, were among 8,000 bones found in a mass "graveyard" near Cuenca, southwest of Teruel, Spain, in 2007. Discovered by railroad workers laying a new track, the fossils date from about 70 million years ago—close to the end of the dinosaurs' reign.

DIG DEEPER

DINÓPOLIS WORLD

Dinópolis World is not just one but six museums scattered around Teruel, Spain. Each has different displays of fossils and replica dinosaurs. Titania in Riodeva focuses on *Turiasaurus*, and the main museum in Teruel has 500 dinosaur exhibits, including an alarmingly realistic robot *Tyrannosaurus*! The Dinópolis staff are at the forefront of research, so they're a mine of information about local fossil sites and what you might find.

Femur

No joke!

What looks a little like a pelican and has 220 teeth? Nothing anyone had ever seen before, Spanish dinosaur hunters thought, on finding a fossil like that in Las Hoyas in 1993. They named their new dinosaur *Pelecanimimus* —"pelican mimic"—and figured out it scooted around on its two powerful back legs in the early Cretaceous. Exactly why it had so many teeth remains a mystery, especially because other dinosaurs of its type— the ornithomimosaurs, or ostrich dinosaurs— usually had none!

Pelecanimimus

GETTING YOUR BEARINGS

When you land in the Triassic, you find yourself in an entirely different world. It's hot, and much of the landscape is dry and dusty. There are no flowers anywhere and no grass. You recognize some smaller creatures—hey, there's a dragonfly! And others look vaguely familiar—could that be a giant crocodile? But some are breathtakingly bizarre, and others are kind of scary!

Catch the drift?

At least in the Triassic you always know where you are: Pangaea. Right now, all of Earth's landmasses are joined together to form this one supercontinent. It stretches from the Northern Hemisphere to the Southern Hemisphere. Yet despite its vast size, there's little variety in its climate or landscapes.

Pangaea

Continents today

Watch out for wandering dinosaurs.

Travel early or late in the day to avoid the full heat of the Sun.

Lie of the land

The interior of Pangaea is dry and dusty. There are few mountain ranges or river valleys, so you can see far ahead as you trudge across this desert. Salt lakes shimmer in the distance. The sweat's pouring off you. But, following a streambed, you start to find some plants sprouting in the stony ground, then spot a line of trees on the horizon. Shade at last! You've reached the coast. You see clusters of towering pine trees and what look like reeds and ferns growing near the water's edge. You hear an occasional roar and screech, and rustling in the shrubbery. Clearly there's much more life here!

Follow waterways downstream to reach the coast.

WEATHER EYE

Hot, isn't it? The early Triassic was a period of global warming, and Pangaea is centered on the equator, the part of the world that receives the most direct sunlight. In many places it's often a steady, energy-sapping 100°F (38°C).

Don't forget to wear a broad-brimmed hat, slurp down plenty of water, and keep slapping on that sunscreen!

Scan the horizon for greenery.

LET'S HIT THE BEACH!

Coastal areas are lined with forest and swamps.

Pterosaurs

THE TRIASSIC SCENE

At the end of the previous geological period, the Permian, rapid climate change caused a near-total mass extinction—about 95 percent of all creatures were wiped out. So, in the Triassic, life is just starting to get going again.

TALL TREES

Take a closer look at the trees around you. Huge, aren't they? Most look a little like big pine trees or conifers. Recognize that one over there with the long, spiky branches? It's a monkey-puzzle tree, still around in your day. And this one here with the fan-shaped leaves? That's a ginkgo, or maidenhair tree, which grows in modern-day China and Japan.

Ginkgo tree—
It has tough,
waxy leaves for
protection.

Cycad
palm

HEAD HIGH

The smaller, palmlike trees that you see everywhere are called cycads. And the ones that look like clumps of furry spears are called *Pleuromeia*. They sprout all over the Triassic world, too.

Horsetails

Pleuromeia

Ferns

LOWER STORY

At ground level most of the greenery is ferns. Those plants that look like bamboo are horsetails, a type of plant that will be widespread throughout the Mesozoic Era. But no matter how hard you look, you won't see any grass—it didn't grow until long after the dinosaurs. There are no flowers, but you won't have to wait quite as long to see them again.

Ferns

Monkey-
puzzle
tree

Eudimorphodon

First flight

Raise your eyes to the skies and take a closer look at what you might have thought were birds. These are actually flying reptiles, or pterosaurs—the first bony creatures ever to take to the air. That one up there is *Eudimorphodon*, and it's about the size of a seagull.

Offshore

There are no dinosaurs underwater. But there are giant aquatic reptiles, including some called nothosaurs, which, like seals, dive to catch fish and then haul themselves out onto the shore to bask on rocks. One of the most bizarre creatures of the Triassic is *Tanystropheus*, whose 10-ft. (3-m) neck is longer than its body and tail combined.

Tanystropheus

DO YOU THINK THEY'D LIKE A MARSHMALLOW?

After dark

Some little critters will be familiar, including dragonflies, frogs, and cockroaches. Early in the day or last thing at night, keep a lookout for small, furry creatures such as *Morganucodon*, one of the first mammals—and one of your oldest ancestors!

Morganucodon

FIELD GUIDE:
STARTING SMALL

You can use this handy "field guide" to identify the dinosaurs that you see on your trip. At this point they're still far outnumbered by other reptiles or reptile-like creatures, so picking them out from the crowd can be tricky!

On the rise

Look for small reptiles running on two legs and moving in groups. These were among the first dinosaurs to appear on Earth, and the oldest known species, *Eoraptor,* is only about the size of a dog. Mostly lizard-hipped meat eaters, or theropods, these guys feed on small creatures such as lizards and mammals, or scavenge dead animals.

Eoraptor   *Saltopus*

Perfect pet?

Some of these little guys are pretty cute, aren't they? You might even be eyeing one up as a pet. But before you drag one home, consider the drawbacks:

Even the smallest dinosaurs need a lot of space to run around. And they're pretty hard to keep up with.

Dinosaurs were not the smartest creatures, so training one is going to be a major challenge. Sit and fetch? No chance. House training? Forget it.

They get through a lot of lizards. Are you happy to provide a steady supply?

Forget how cute it is—look how many teeth it has! Look at those razor-sharp claws! Get on the bad side of even the tiniest dinosaur and it could start ripping you to shreds.

Having second thoughts now?

Procompsognathus   Herrerasaurus   Coelophysis

WHAT DID I DO TO DESERVE THIS?

Here come the herbivores!

Some of the biggest creatures that you'll see around you are probably (and fortunately!) plant-eating dinosaurs. Such as that huge one rising above the trees, *Plateosaurus*, or that little one walking on its hind legs, *Thecodontosaurus*.

Plateosaurus rises onto its hind legs to feed on foliage other dinosaurs can't reach.

Hyperodapedon

LOW PROFILE

The most common plant eaters of the Triassic, though you might not notice them at first, are not dinosaurs but rhynchosaurs—small, low-slung reptiles with flat, triangular heads and beaklike jaws. Watch closely and you'll see them use their prominent tusks to rip up plants.

Placerias does a good impersonation of a reptile but is a synapsid— a cousin of the mammals.

Thecodontosaurus

FIELD GUIDE:
WHO'S THE BOSS?

So who's in charge around here? Which creatures rule the roost? Well it's not the dinosaurs—yet. Though some larger dinosaur predators are starting to throw their weight around, the really big guys in town are the crocodilian archosaurs, a far more common bunch of reptiles.

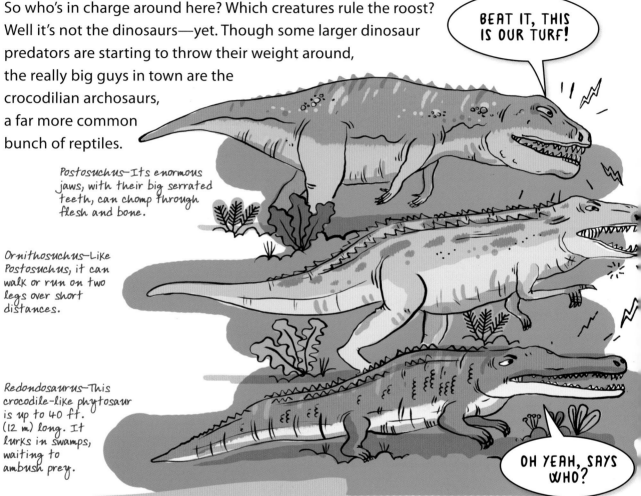

> BEAT IT, THIS IS OUR TURF!

Postosuchus—Its enormous jaws, with their big serrated teeth, can chomp through flesh and bone.

Ornithosuchus—Like *Postosuchus*, it can walk or run on two legs over short distances.

Redondosaurus—This crocodile-like phytosaur is up to 40 ft. (12 m) long. It lurks in swamps, waiting to ambush prey.

> OH YEAH, SAYS WHO?

The old guard

Dinosaurs are a branch of a much larger reptile group, the archosaurs, which spread across Pangaea during the Early Triassic. The archosaurs quickly muscled in on most territories and now hold sway as the supercontinent's major predators. At the top are the crocodilian archosaurs, which include *Postosuchus*, *Ornithosuchus*, and the especially crocodile-like phytosaurs. Not huge by later dinosaur standards but powerful and armed with massive jaws and sharp claws, they're a force to be reckoned with and are always on the hunt for flesh—so watch out!

RACE FOR YOUR LIFE

What if you're chased by one of the big predators, such as *Postosuchus* or *Gojirasaurus*? Think you could outrun them? Hmm. If you get a head start on *Postosuchus*, which could reach speeds of 15 mph (25 km/h) over a short distance, you might just get clear. But it's thought that *Gojirasaurus* could zip along at 22 mph (35 km/h). Oh dear. Time for another strategy!

New kids on the block

WE'RE MOVING IN!

As dinosaurs get bigger, they're starting to assert themselves. Among the pushier predators are *Gojirasaurus* and *Liliensternus*, two of the largest meat eaters of the Late Triassic. Their long back legs make them frighteningly fast, and both are big and strong enough to bring down a giant plant eater such as *Plateosaurus*.

Gojirasaurus—Has a muscular neck and tail, powerful forelimbs, and razor-sharp teeth.

YUM!

MOVIE MONSTER

Gojirasaurus is named after the 1954 Japanese science fiction film *Godzilla*—*Gojira* in Japanese. It tells the story of a giant dinosaur-like monster that rampages through modern-day Japan.

Liliensternus—It can be identified by the two prominent crests on its forehead.

Head for a dense stand of trees, where these big guys will have trouble weaving through the narrow gaps.

TIME'S UP!

Being on the spot for the start of the age of the dinosaurs has been a blast. But with those two terrors on your tail, it seems like a good time to wind the clock forward—and head back home!

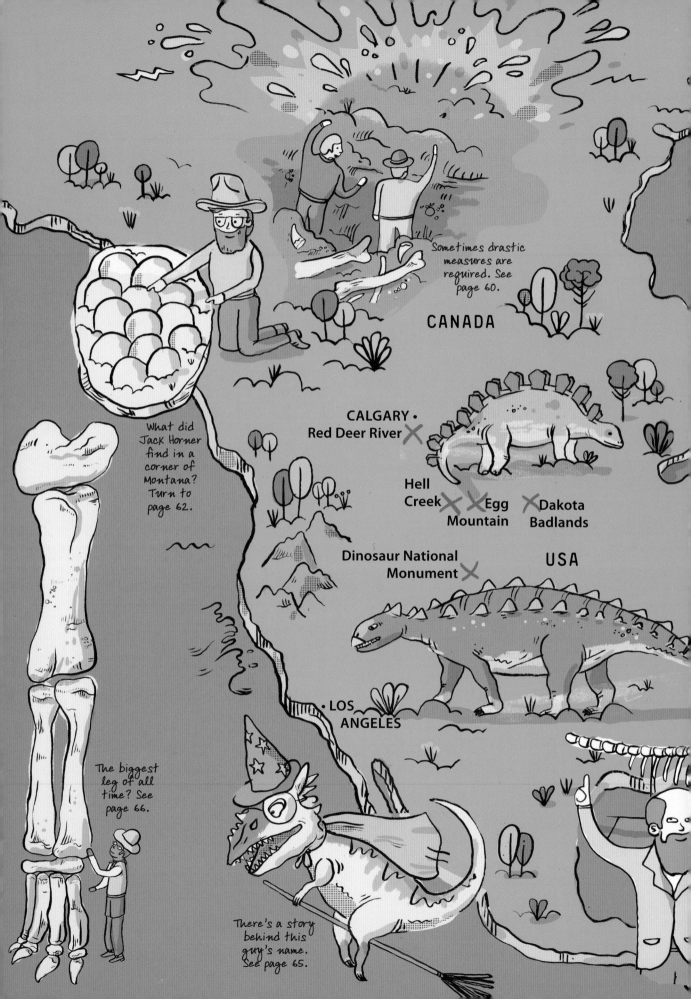

Sometimes drastic measures are required. See page 60.

CANADA

CALGARY •
Red Deer River ✕

Hell
Creek ✕ ✕ Egg
Mountain   ✕ Dakota
Badlands

Dinosaur National
Monument ✕

USA

• LOS
ANGELES

What did Jack Horner find in a corner of Montana? Turn to page 62.

The biggest leg of all time? See page 66.

There's a story behind this guy's name. See page 65.

Is this the ultimate dinosaur hunter's trophy? Turn to page 61.

He was the hottest hunter of his day. See page 59.

If you go down to this museum at night, you could be in for a surprise. See page 57.

NEW YORK •

WASHINGTON •

One strike and you're out! See page 60.

STARS OF THE WEST

After a day's digging in the barren ranges of the American West, you're ready to head home. You've found fantastic fossils of some of the most famous dinosaurs, including an awesome Triceratops horn, which you've stowed carefully in your bag. It took you hours to get here, through a maze of steep-sided gullies and canyons, and it's going to be a long hike home. Daylight is fading, and you can see that it's raining higher up in the mountains. Better move fast. But where did you put that map? And where's that sound of rushing water coming from? Uh-oh. Time to make for higher ground!

Head or tail? What started this famous feud? Answers on page 54.

HUNTER'S QUEST

Head in the right direction and you'll find fossils galore in North America. It not only has a vast range of sites from the Triassic, Jurassic, and Cretaceous periods but is also the land of the most famous dinosaurs. Can you score some superstar fossils?

Go west, young dinosaur hunter! Dinosaurs lived all over North America. But, because of the way the continent developed after they disappeared, most of the Mesozoic rocks are in the western interior.

Go west!

ROCKY MOUNTAINS

LET'S DIG HERE!

APPALACHIAN MOUNTAINS

GREAT PLAINS

The uplifting of the Rocky Mountains between 80 and 55 million years ago wrecked many Mesozoic layers.

Mesozoic rocks and dinosaur fossils lie near the surface here.

The Great Plains were flooded in the Mesozoic, so most fossils here are marine fossils.

Ice-age glaciers bulldozed Mesozoic rocks off most of the East.

WISH I'D BROUGHT MY GPS!

Navigating the Badlands

In the western interior—from Alberta in Canada down to New Mexico in the southwestern United States—sediments slowly settled over dinosaur remains, creating bands of fossil-rich rocks. Since then, rivers have cut deep into these layers, in places forming mazes of canyons among steep-sided, flat-topped hills—now prime fossil-hunting territory. Because they were hard to cross and easy to get lost in, early travelers called these landscapes "badlands," and you still have to be careful there today.

Take a good map and compass, and always tell someone where you are going.

A rich seam

Among North America's richest Mesozoic layers for dinosaur hunters is the Morrison Formation, a thick bed of Late Jurassic rock that covers 600,000 sq. mi. (1.5 million sq km), from southwestern Canada south to New Mexico.

Look for a band of green or gray stone in layers of redder rocks.

TO MY FANS, T. REX

Best wishes, Steg

Dino-stars

There's no disputing that *Tyrannosaurus* is America's biggest dino-star. Huge at the box office, it has appeared in movies ranging from *King Kong* to *Jurassic Park*. Even though it lived in a different period, *Stegosaurus* often plays a supporting role in movies and is also a regular on television and in cartoons.

Sedimentary rock layers

Deep, eroded canyons

DESERT DANGERS

North America's western interior can be baking hot in the summer and bitterly cold in the winter—so be prepared! A danger in canyon country is flash flooding. After sudden, heavy downpours, water may rush through gorges, sweeping branches, stones, boulders—and possibly unfortunate dinosaur hunters—downstream. Avoid canyons when heavy rain is expected, and make sure that you've scouted a quick way up to safety.

Watch out for rattlesnakes and scorpions.

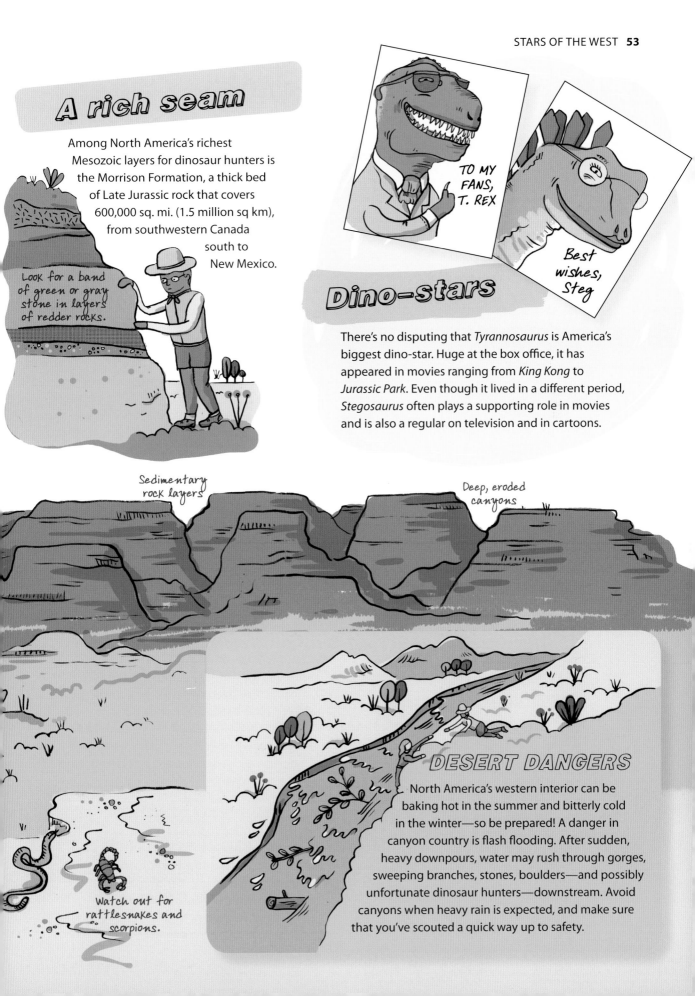

THE BONE WARS

When "dino-mania" hit North America in the 1850s, determined dinosaur hunters snatched up every fossil they could find for museums and private collections. And in the 1870s two collectors started a feud more vicious than a hungry *T. rex*.

Turning tail?

When they met in 1868, Edward Cope, a wealthy collector, and Othniel Marsh, curator of Yale University's Museum of Natural History, had a fine old time together. But soon they were bitter rivals. Some say the turning point was when Marsh bribed fossil hunters to send finds only to him, and Cope found out. Others say it was when Cope reconstructed the skeleton of an *Elasmosaurus*, an aquatic reptile, but placed the skull on the tail—and Marsh took delight in reporting his error far and wide. Either way, from the early 1870s, the gloves were off!

Duel in the West

In what became known as the Bone Wars, Cope and Marsh started trying to outdo each other by naming as many new dinosaurs as possible. Both led expeditions to the American West. When the parties crossed paths, they spied on each other, tried to steal each other's specimens, and even threw rocks at each other. Once back home, Cope and Marsh wrote spiteful articles attacking each other's discoveries. It wasn't exactly dignified, but the public loved it!

YOU NEED *YOUR* HEAD EXAMINED IF YOU THINK THAT'S RIGHT!

Cope must have thought he had trumped everyone in 1877 when he discovered the fossilized bone of what's still one of the biggest known dinosaurs, *Amphicoelias fragilimus* (see page 10).

SCORECARD: MARSH

- ☑ 300 papers published
- ☑ 500 new animal species named
- ☑ 80 new dinosaurs named
- ☑ Wealthy, respected, living in a huge mansion

And the winner is . . . ?

SCORECARD: COPE

- ☑ 1,400 papers published
- ☑ 1,200 new animal species named
- ☑ 56 new dinosaurs named
- ☒ Penniless, living in one room in a boardinghouse

The result of the Bone Wars was a win for science. Between them Cope and Marsh discovered 136 new dinosaur species, including many of today's most famous dinosaurs, such as *Stegosaurus*, *Triceratops*, and *Diplodocus*. Cope scored well when it came to publishing papers, but his lavish spending left him a ruined man.

DIG DEEPER

THE AMERICAN MUSEUM OF NATURAL HISTORY

The cities of eastern North America might be far from the action when it comes to *finding* dinosaurs. But they are where most of the best fossils end up, and they have some of the world's most spectacular displays of dinosaur remains.

Allosaurus

Barosaurus

IMAGINE WHAT A BATTLE THIS WOULD HAVE BEEN!

STANDING TALL

When in 1895 Edward Cope finally had to sell his private treasure chest of more than 10,000 fossils, it became the basis of the new fossil collection of the American Museum of Natural History (AMNH) in New York. Today the AMNH has the largest dinosaur fossil collection in the world. Its most dramatic exhibit shows three skeletons arranged in a lifelike scene: a towering *Barosaurus* rearing up to protect a young one against a rampaging *Allosaurus*.

AARGH!

A NIGHT AT THE MUSEUM

The AMNH was the setting for the first *Night at the Museum* movie, and you can actually arrange to stay overnight at the AMNH, viewing fossils by flashlight—spooky!— and sleeping among the displays.

CATCH UP WITH ME AGAIN ON PAGE 108.

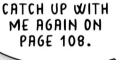

WILD TIMES

The AMNH's collection grew rapidly in the early 1900s, thanks to the work of several adventurous dinosaur hunters. One of the most famous and successful was Roy Chapman Andrews. A brilliant scientist, Andrews was also a tough, fearless explorer—and a crack shot. Just like you'll do, he traveled the world in search of the best fossils and museum treasures, experiencing remarkable adventures along the way— the Indiana Jones of his day!

RIVAL COLLECTION

Late in life, feuding dinosaur collector Othniel Marsh became curator of vertebrate fossils at the new US National Museum. When he died, the fossils he had gathered on behalf of the museum—all 80 tons (72 tonnes) of them!— were transferred to a museum in Washington, DC, now known as the Smithsonian National Museum of Natural History.

RULED BY THE RIVER

Ready to get wet? Canada's top fossil site is a two-and-a-half-hour drive southeast of the western city of Calgary, in the valley of the Red Deer River. It's easy enough to get there, but to fully explore the fossil-rich valley you might need to do what early dinosaur hunters did—take to the water.

BARGING IN

In 1910 one of the greatest dinosaur hunters of all time, Barnum Brown, decided to explore the Red Deer River more closely. To do that, he had to travel by boat, so he built a wide, flat barge to carry his provisions and specimens and set off down the winding river. In 1912 he found himself sharing the waterway with a rival group of fossil hunters, Charles Sternberg and his three young sons, traveling on their own raft. The race was on!

HEY, THAT WAS MY IDEA!

The rafts carried all supplies, tools, and fossils.

Killer Canuck

The first major find on the Red Deer River was made by Canadian dinosaur hunter Joseph Tyrrell in 1884, when he was just twenty-six years old. He dug up the skull of a fearsome Cretaceous meat eater, later named *Albertosaurus* after the province in which it was discovered.

The parties soon agreed to dig in different areas.

KING OF COLLECTORS

For many admirers, Barnum Brown was the "King of Collectors." Over several decades he scoured North America and other parts of the world, discovering a spectacular range of fossils, including the first *Tyrannosaurus* remains. Brown's parents named him after the circus owner P. T. Barnum, and there was always something of the showman about him. He even had his own radio show—about dinosaurs, of course.

Brown liked to wear a shirt, tie, hat, and full-length fur coat—even in baking-hot deserts. How cool is that?!

Spiky specimen

YOU COULD GET HOOKED ON ME!

Among Sternberg's major discoveries on the Red Deer River was a spectacular horned dinosaur, *Styracosaurus*. The name means "spiked lizard."

A 17-mi. (27-km) stretch of the Red Deer River has yielded 300 dinosaur skeletons—more than any other fossil site!

CAN WE ACTUALLY STEER THIS THING?!

DIG DEEPER

• •

ROYAL TYRRELL MUSEUM

The Red Deer River valley is now part of Dinosaur Provincial Park, which organizes regular dinosaur digs and fossil prospecting trips. And just two hours' drive northwest, in Drumheller, is the Royal Tyrrell Museum, Canada's major museum of paleontology, which houses many of the Red Deer River finds. Here you can view re-creations of scenes from the Canadian Cretaceous and visit the Preparation Lab to watch paleontologists working on newly discovered fossils.

Caught off guard

I KNEW WE SHOULD HAVE LEARNED TO SWIM!

In the late 20th century huge beds containing thousands of fossils of a horned dinosaur called *Centrosaurus* were found by the river. It's thought that the creatures died together as an enormous herd tried to cross a river in full flood.

RISING FROM HELL

Hell Creek: it's not the most inviting name, is it? But this river valley in the badlands of Montana has been a favorite dinosaur-hunter destination since the early 1900s. And from its infernal depths have emerged some of the most awe-inspiring creatures of all time.

Having a blast

LUCKY THOSE BONES ARE TOUGH!

Before he went rafting on the Red Deer River (see p. 58), renowned fossil hunter Barnum Brown spent three years exploring at Hell Creek. In 1902 he found traces of huge dinosaurs. Over the next six years he collected parts of the skeleton of what was clearly a colossal predator, including 12-in. (30-cm) teeth and a skull that weighed more than 1,000 lb. (450 kg). He sent the fossils by train to his employer, the American Museum of Natural History in New York, where a skeleton was assembled and named *Tyrannosaurus rex*—the "tyrant-lizard king."

To get to fossils, Brown used dynamite to blast apart whole hillsides.

TAKING NO CHANCES

In 1906 Brown's team also discovered the first fossils of *Ankylosaurus*, a Late Cretaceous herbivore, at Hell Creek. As big as a car and built like a tank, *Ankylosaurus* was covered in thick, armor-like plates of bone and cloaked with tough skin studded with nodules and spikes. At the end of its tail was a broad, heavy club that could break the bones of anything that got in its way. You needed that kind of protection when *Tyrannosaurus* was around!

Watch out for that tail!

DIG DEEPER

• •

MONTANA DINOSAUR TRAIL

If you're a *Tyrannosaurus* fan, don't miss the Museum of the Rockies in Bozeman, Montana. It has 13 *Tyrannosaurus* specimens—the biggest collection in the world—including one of only two complete skeletons ever found ("Big Mike") and the largest known *Tyrannosaurus* skull ("Custer"). You can even join a Dinosaur Detectives or Jr. Paleontologists summer camp. And from the museum you can follow the Montana Dinosaur Trail to 13 other dinosaur-related museums, parks, and sites. Hope you've planned a long stay!

THREE-PRONGED DEFENSE

How about a nice, three-horned *Triceratops* skull to hang on your wall? Well, you've got a great chance of finding one here: between the years 2000 and 2010, no fewer than 47 were found at Hell Creek. A hulky herbivore with unmistakable headgear, *Triceratops* plodded around in the Late Cretaceous, grazing on shrubs and doing its best to steer clear of its major predator, *Tyrannosaurus*. Many fossils discovered here show signs of deadly battles between these two giants.

Tyrannosaurus liked to chomp on Triceratops's frill.

Triceratops gouged upward with its lethal horns.

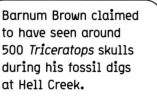

Barnum Brown claimed to have seen around 500 *Triceratops* skulls during his fossil digs at Hell Creek.

SCRAMBLED EGGS

They've been cracked, crushed, scrambled, and splattered in rock layers all over the world and occasionally found fossilized. But until the late 20th century few paleontologists paid dinosaur eggs much attention. That all changed after a remarkable discovery in 1978 on the Two Medicine Formation in northwestern Montana—often referred to as "Egg Mountain."

Maiasaura and other dinosaurs hatched their eggs and then fed the hatchlings until they were ready to leave the nest.

AW, NOT FERNS AGAIN!

Shop talk

It started in a shop—a rock and fossil shop in Bynum, Montana. Dinosaur hunter Jack Horner was browsing the displays and noticed bones of a baby hadrosaur, a Cretaceous plant eater. He asked the store owner, Marion Brandvold, where she had found them and, on exploring the site with his digging partner, Bob Makela, found the bones of 15 more baby dinosaurs surrounded by fossilized eggs. Clearly this was a dinosaur nest.

Fossilized nest

A gentler side

You might wonder why a nest was such a big deal. Well, these were the first dinosaur eggs to be discovered in the Americas. What's more, while paleontologists had previously assumed that dinosaurs simply laid eggs and left them to hatch on their own, this nest showed that the hatchlings stayed in the nest for some time while feeding. And that meant that these dinosaurs took care of their young. Suddenly a gentler side to dinosaurs was revealed! So Horner called the new species *Maiasaura*, meaning "good mother lizard."

"Big" Jack Horner was the expert consultant on the *Jurassic Park* movies and the inspiration for the character of Alan Grant.

Take a crack?

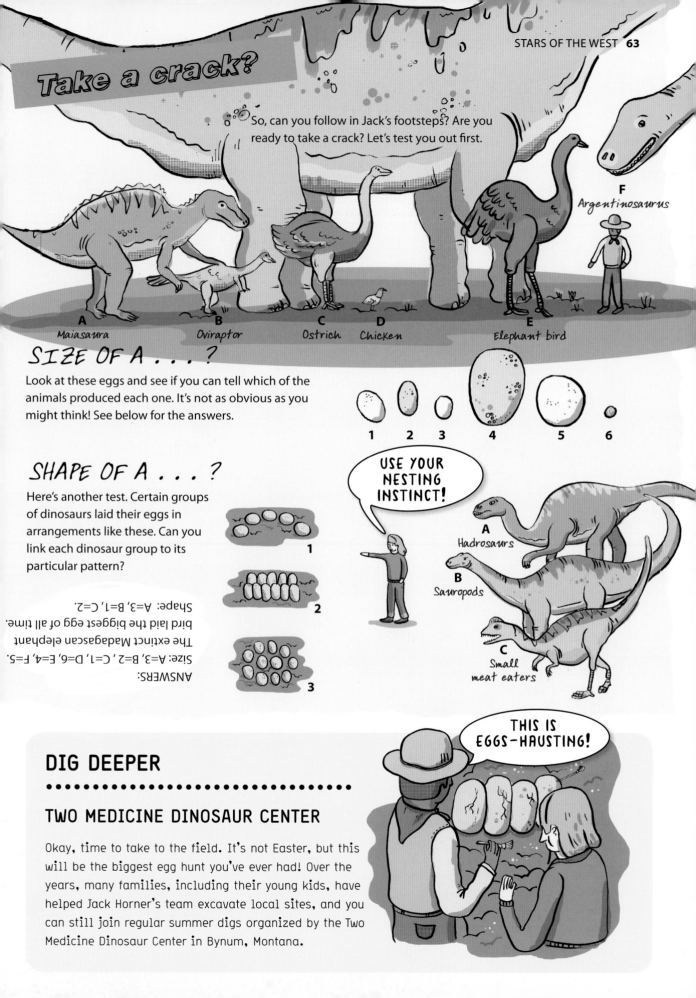

So, can you follow in Jack's footsteps? Are you ready to take a crack? Let's test you out first.

A Maiasaura
B Oviraptor
C Ostrich
D Chicken
E Elephant bird
F Argentinosaurus

SIZE OF A . . . ?

Look at these eggs and see if you can tell which of the animals produced each one. It's not as obvious as you might think! See below for the answers.

1 2 3 4 5 6

SHAPE OF A . . . ?

Here's another test. Certain groups of dinosaurs laid their eggs in arrangements like these. Can you link each dinosaur group to its particular pattern?

1

2

3

USE YOUR NESTING INSTINCT!

A Hadrosaurs

B Sauropods

C Small meat eaters

ANSWERS:
Size: A=3, B=2 , C=1, D=6, E=4, F=5.
The extinct Madagascan elephant bird laid the biggest egg of all time.
Shape: A=3, B=1, C=2.

THIS IS EGGS-HAUSTING!

DIG DEEPER

• •

TWO MEDICINE DINOSAUR CENTER

Okay, time to take to the field. It's not Easter, but this will be the biggest egg hunt you've ever had! Over the years, many families, including their young kids, have helped Jack Horner's team excavate local sites, and you can still join regular summer digs organized by the Two Medicine Dinosaur Center in Bynum, Montana.

GAME CHANGERS

It's one thing to uncover a dinosaur fossil. It's another to find one that reveals something new about dinosaurs. That's been the case with several finds from North and South Dakota. Can you add to this remarkable record?

A new impression

In 1964 John Ostrom discovered the bones of a small Cretaceous predator called *Deinonychus*. At the time, people thought of dinosaurs as slow, stupid, and scaly. But on studying the fossils, Ostrom realized that, in order to survive, *Deinonychus* must have run quickly on two legs and hunted in packs. That meant that it had to be fast, agile, *and* pretty smart.

A dinosaur named Sue

Scientists still aren't sure if Sue was female or male!

THAT'S MY GIRL! I THINK.

Scouring the Black Hills of South Dakota in 1990, Sue Hendrickson unearthed an amazing fossil: the most complete *Tyrannosaurus* ever found. Named "Sue" in her honor, it revealed fascinating details about the lives of these colossal predators. Studies of the bones indicated that Sue had survived broken ribs, a torn tendon, and various diseases. And examinations of the brain cavity showed that Sue had highly developed senses of sight, balance, and smell—useful for sniffing out, spotting, and then chasing prey.

NO, IT'S MY DINOSAUR!

As soon as Sue was found, a huge argument erupted over who owned the bones. Was it the finders, the farmer who owned the land, or the government? Finally, in 1995, a court ruled in favor of the farmer. When the skeleton was put up for sale, it sold for $8.36 million— still the highest price ever paid for a fossil.

Re-assembled, Sue now inhabits the Field Museum in Chicago and is very well cared for in her very old age.

REALLY, I'M WORTH IT!

SPECIAL OFFER
$8,360,000

Deinonychus

Ostrom also suggested that Deinonychus might have had feathers.

Tenontosaurus

Back from the dead

Tyler Lyson began fossil hunting on his uncle's North Dakota farm at age twelve, and at sixteen, in 1999, he found a fossil of a duck-billed hadrosaur he named "Dakota." But it wasn't until 2006, after training as a paleontologist, that he went back to excavate it. When he did, he realized it was a rare find: a dinosaur with fossilized organs, tissues, and skin.

Tyler set up Marmarth Research Foundation to involve the public in paleontology. You can sign up for one of his digs.

People said (incorrectly) that Tyler's fossil was "mummified," and it became known as the "Dinosaur Mummy"!

A WIZARD IDEA

Sue was named after its finder, and Dakota after the place where it was found. If you found a new dinosaur, would you name it after yourself? Your mom? Or maybe your favorite book? When three amateur fossil hunters gave a South Dakota dinosaur skull to the Children's Museum of Indianapolis, the museum called the new species _Dracorex hogwartsia_, after Hogwarts—the school that features in the Harry Potter books.

PICTURES ON THE WALL

You've probably gathered cratefuls of Cretaceous fossils by now. So it's time to head south to the boneyards on the Utah-Colorado border—the world's richest source of Late Jurassic finds.

On display

To get a sense of this region's treasures, check out the incredible wall of bones in the Quarry Center at Dinosaur National Monument near Jensen, Utah. Here paleontologists have excavated a sandstone cliff to expose more than 1,500 dinosaur bones. The creatures probably died along a waterway at various times, and their remains were washed downstream, settling together in one spot.

Sauropod selection

Camarasaurus—no fossilized tennis rackets have yet been found.

NOT MUCH ROOM FOR A PASSING SHOT!

The Quarry Center bones are from a mix of species, including *Stegosaurus* and several giant sauropods—long-necked plant eaters of the Jurassic—such as *Diplodocus* and *Apatosaurus*. The skulls that you'll see are those of another sauropod, *Camarasaurus*. More than half the length of a tennis court, it was the most common herbivore of the North American Jurassic.

JUST PULLING YOUR LEG!

Jim's giants

Jensen estimated Ultrasauros's weight at 200 tons (180 tonnes). A shoulder blade that he found was 8 ft. (2.4 m) long.

Make sure that you've got plenty of luggage space, because the bones dug up here include some of the biggest ever found. In the 1970s Jim Jensen unearthed colossal bones that appeared to belong to three gargantuan sauropods that he named *Ultrasauros*, *Supersaurus*, and *Dystylosaurus*. Based on these scraps, *Supersaurus* could have been as tall as a five-story building and as long as an Olympic-size swimming pool.

GETTING IT STRAIGHT

A pile of bones won't always paint a clear picture. When Othniel Marsh found the first *Stegosaurus* fossil near Morrison, Colorado, in 1877, the fossils were a jumbled mess and the large triangular plates near the creature's back bones were a real puzzle. At first Marsh thought they might have lain flat, forming a shell like that of a turtle, and that *Stegosaurus* might even have been a water dweller. But in 1885 another *Stegosaurus* was found. Usefully, it was almost complete, lying sideways, and squashed flat—and it showed that the plates were not horizontal but stood up vertically on *Stegosaurus*'s back.

The flattened Stegosaurus found in 1885 became known as the "roadkill fossil."

OH NO!

Bottom of the class?

Because dinosaurs have very small brains relative to the size of their bodies, it was thought for a long time that they must all have been dim-witted. But although they weren't the smartest of creatures, there were some brighter sparks among them.

WISH I COULD READ HIS WRITING!

YUM—A TWIG!

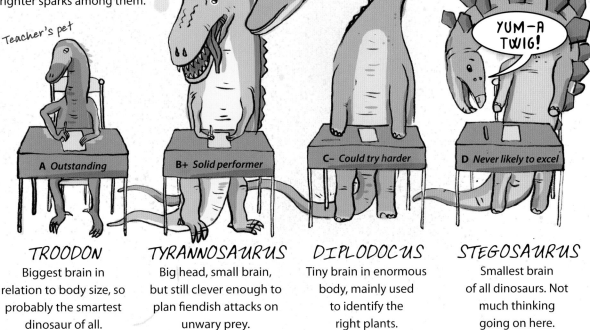

Teacher's pet

A *Outstanding*   **B+** *Solid performer*   **C−** *Could try harder*   **D** *Never likely to excel*

TROODON
Biggest brain in relation to body size, so probably the smartest dinosaur of all.

TYRANNOSAURUS
Big head, small brain, but still clever enough to plan fiendish attacks on unwary prey.

DIPLODOCUS
Tiny brain in enormous body, mainly used to identify the right plants.

STEGOSAURUS
Smallest brain of all dinosaurs. Not much thinking going on here.

Could the Amazon jungle still be a dinosaur hideout? Learn more on page 71.

BRAZIL

Going up? But what? And where? Find out on page 71.

BOLIVIA

• SUCRE

Swamp dwellers have resurfaced in southern deserts. See page 74.

Valley of the Moon

CHILE

Touch down here and the sky's the limit. Turn to page 74.

Nuequén

BUENOS AIRES

ARGENTINA

A bridge too far? This land will test your appetite for adventure!

He separated the dinosaur from the goats. See page 75.

on't let this guy get on your nerves. See page 73.

What's with the crazy headgear? Get to the bottom of it on page 71.

A NEW FRONTIER

Digging on a bone-dry ridge of the Andes Mountains of western South America, you make a startling discovery: a huge chunk of a sauropod thighbone. Getting this monster find back to base camp is going to be quite a challenge. Helped by your buddy, you manage to cart it down the narrow path. But then, as you recross the old rope bridge, the extra weight causes the bridge to sag alarmingly. Ropes start snapping, the bridge is tilting, there's 650 ft. (200 m) of nothing but air below you. Do you sacrifice your precious find and sprint for safety or take a deep breath and hold steady as you go?

He's got a whole dinosaur in his hands. See page 72.

Meet a world leader among dinosaur hunters on page 72.

HUNTER'S QUEST

In dinosaur terms, South America is a happening place! Little explored by paleontologists until recently, it has been the source of many exciting modern-day discoveries, including fossils of some of the oldest, smallest, and biggest known species. Can you get in on the action?

Diplodocus—uh, what?!

A new frontier

Based on what's been found so far, your best bet is to head for the open spaces of the south or the mountainous fringes of the northeast and northwest. Little has been discovered in the vast jungle realm of the Amazon. Not surprising really. It's hard enough to hack a way through the undergrowth there, let alone start digging. Plus you have a whole lot of other things to worry about: jaguars, gigantic bone-crushing snakes, giant spiders, even poisonous frogs. But this could be an untapped source of startling new finds. Are you brave enough for a jungle jaunt?

Boa constrictor

Jaguar

Poison dart frog

Tarantula

Hanging around?

You might even find more than you bargained for. Native peoples have long told stories of dinosaur-like reptiles surviving deep in the jungle. And in 1907 English explorer Percy Fawcett thought he saw the head of a *Diplodocus* rising above treetops, as well as "monstrous tracks of unknown origin." Inspired by this, Sir Arthur Conan Doyle, author of the Sherlock Holmes stories, published a novel in 1912 called *The Lost World*, about an expedition to a remote Amazonian plateau where dinosaurs still exist.

DRAT! THEY FOUND US!

No picnic

If you want to play it safe, stick to the southern grasslands, known as the pampas, and the nearby deserts. But exploring here will be no picnic either. Although the weather isn't too bad, many fossil sites lie in remote, rugged realms with little shelter and far from towns and stores. Better bring everything you need!

JUNGLE GIANT

One of the few finds from the northern jungles is *Amazonsaurus*, a small sauropod, or long-necked plant eater, that lived about 100 million years ago.

Tupuxuara

> WONDER HOW LONG IT TOOK THEM TO THINK UP MY NAME?!

Tupuxuara skull

Fly zone

Feel like filling out your fossil collection with some flying reptiles? Then head for the Araripe Plateau in northeastern Brazil. No fewer than 19 new pterosaur species have been found there. The biggest, *Tupuxuara*, had a wingspan of 20 ft. (6 m) and a spectacular head crest, as is clear from its bizarre skull.

This way up

At Cal Orck'o, outside Sucre, Bolivia, you can view the world's largest collection of dinosaur tracks. There are more than 5,000 prints and 462 trackways, made by dozens of Late Cretaceous species. Discovered by quarry workers, the tracks climb a near-vertical limestone wall. At some point in more recent times, the rock layers were tipped upward by earth movements.

> WHERE ON EARTH WERE THEY GOING?

POINTING THE WAY

From the 1960s onward, a small group of pioneering paleontologists put South America well and truly on the dinosaur hunter's map—and blazed a trail for you to follow.

Carnotaurus may have used its horns in fights with members of its own species.

Follow the leader

Though not related to the famous French emperor Napoleon Bonaparte, José is a born leader!

The man who has done the most to map out the South American Mesozoic is José Bonaparte, the so-called Master of the Mesozoic. As a boy growing up on the plains south of Buenos Aires, Argentina, in the 1930s, he scoured the grasslands for fossils. He has since discovered and named at least 25 new dinosaur species.

PINT SIZE

Among Bonaparte's first and most important finds were some of the smallest dinosaur skeletons ever seen. They came from a clutch of eggs and babies unearthed in the far south of Argentina in 1977. Bonaparte called the new Triassic species *Mussaurus patagonicus*—"Patagonian mouse lizard." Find one and you could hold the entire skeleton in the palms of your hands.

Mussaurus skeleton

IT LOOKS NOTHING LIKE ME!

Dino-taur

Bonaparte has made some much bigger catches too. One of the biggest was *Carnotaurus*, which he found in Chubut, in central southern Argentina, in 1985. This huge Late Cretaceous predator was up to 30 ft. (9 m) long and crowned with two short horns—hence its name, "meat-eating bull." Its arms were even tinier and weirder than those of other large predators like *Tyrannosaurus*. And its skin was covered in armor-like plates dotted with bony studs. That's one scary sight!

DIG DEEPER

• •

NATURAL SCIENCE MUSEUM, MERCEDES

When José Bonaparte was just nineteen, he and a group of friends in his home town of Mercedes, Argentina, set up a museum to house their fossil collections. It opened to the public in 1965, and you can still visit it today.

Prehistoric pest!

Professional dinosaur hunters usually appear pretty cool, but they can get grumpy at times. In 1996 a man in Brazil took an Early Cretaceous fossil to some paleontologists. Eventually they figured out that he had altered the fossil to make it look like that of a pterosaur, because such fossils were in demand. On closer inspection they realized that it was actually a new species of large predator. But they were still so annoyed at the man's actions that they called it *Irritator*.

Irritator was up to 26 ft. (8 m) long—as big as a small truck!

Irritator had a so-called tail sail along its back

BOO!

Irritator had a close relative in North Africa, *Spinosaurus* (see page 94). This shows South America was joined to Africa until 100 million years ago.

Mirischia, a small Early Cretaceous theropod

AARGH! HE'S JUST SO ANNOYING!

VALLEY OF THE MOON

South America has turned out to be a Triassic treasure trove and is home to some of the oldest dinosaur fossils ever found. Blast off to the Valley of the Moon and you might get your hands on some. It's not really on the Moon, though, but part of the dry, rugged Ischigualasto Formation in northwestern Argentina.

Lunar landscape

I THINK THAT'S TAKING THINGS A LITTLE TOO FAR!

You'll understand the name as soon as you arrive. Barren slopes, weird rock spires, hardly any greenery, and not a drop of water in sight: it's a lunar landscape!

COME ON CLOUD!

WAITING FOR RAIN

The Valley of the Moon lies close to the southeastern fringe of the Atacama Desert, the driest place in the world. Parts of this region go for years without rain. At least that means you can leave your rain gear at home.

Swamp thing

It's hard to believe that this was once a swampy forest. But that's how it was here during the Late Triassic, when dinosaurs first emerged—fossils of tree trunks and ferns provide the proof. It would have been a treacherous landscape. Lurking by the waterways, for example, ready to pounce on and snap up prey, were colossal crocodilians such as *Saurosuchus*. Yikes!

I'M AS LONG AS FIVE ELEVEN-YEAR-OLD KIDS!

Saurosuchus could run on four legs and was about 23 ft. (7 m) long.

Rock spires like these are known as hoodoos.

Small beginnings

In 1959 Victorino Herrera, a goat farmer, spotted some bones sticking out of a rock. Dinosaur hunter Osvaldo Reig figured out that it was a new species of small carnivorous dinosaur, or theropod, from the Triassic and named it *Herrerasaurus* in honor of its finder. Following on from the discovery of fossils of other tiny Triassic dinosaurs in North America, *Herrerasaurus* helped scientists figure out that most of the first meat eaters were little guys.

THAT'S ONE WEIRD-LOOKING GOAT!

First off the mark?

More proof that many of the first dinosaurs were little came from another exciting discovery, made in 1993 by American fossil hunter Paul Sereno. This was an even smaller primitive meat eater called *Eoraptor*. At the time it was the oldest dinosaur fossil ever found, dating back 230 million years.

I LOOKED A LOT BETTER ON PAGE 46.

Eoraptor was only about 3 ft. (1 m) long. You could hold its skull in one hand.

The Valley of the Moon is the only site in the world where fossils span most of the Triassic period.

LAND OF THE GIANTS

Are you ambitious? Like to think big? If so, Nuequén is the place for you. For in this province in the foothills of the Andes Mountains in western Argentina paleontologists have unearthed evidence of some of the most colossal creatures that ever walked on Earth.

A leg up

Scientists have known since the late 1800s that South America was once home to large, long-necked plant-eating dinosaurs, or sauropods. In 1929 German scientist Friedrich von Huene found two enormous dinosaur leg bones in Nuequén and named the species *Antarctosaurus giganteus*. Based on the size of the bones, this would have been one of the largest dinosaurs ever, weighing as much as 76 tons (69 tonnes)—the weight of 1,000 people!

HOW DO I MEASURE UP?

Super heavyweight

In 1913 Rodolfo Coria from the Carmen Funes Museum in Plaza Huincul found several bones from what seemed to be an even bigger sauropod, which he patriotically named *Argentinosaurus*. With its thighbone standing 8 ft. (2.4 m) tall, its overall length could have been 100 ft. (30 m) and its weight up to 90 tons (100 tonnes).

Sail Spines

WHO KNOWS?!

Which way?

One of the most unusual sauropods found anywhere was unearthed in Nuequén in 1984. Named *Amargasaurus* in 1991, it had lethal-looking spines running all the way along its head, backbone, and tail. These may have provided protection from attack, or they may have been sheathed in plates or sails that were used in displays.

Argentinosaurus skeleton

DIG DEEPER
• • • • • • • • • • • • • • • • • • •
CARMEN FUNES MUSEUM

This museum in the town of Plaza Huincul preserves many of the finds from local fossil sites, including the skeletons of *Argentinosaurus* and *Giganotosaurus*. At Lago Barreales, north of town, you can visit the Proyecto Dino excavation site to watch dinosaur hunters in action.

YOU'LL GET THE LOWDOWN HERE!

It would have taken Argentinosaurus about 40 years to grow to its full, colossal length.

Argentinosaurus may have been the heaviest of all dinosaurs.

Groups of Giganotosaurus ganged up to bring down giant sauropods such as Argentinosaurus.

Mammoth meat eater

Were these giant sauropods so big that they had nothing to fear? Or did they meet their match among the meat eaters? In 1994 a car mechanic, Ruben Carolini, found bones in Nuequén that turned out to belong to a mammoth predator possibly even bigger than *Tyrannosaurus*. Rodolfo Coria named it *Giganotosaurus carolinii*, after its discoverer.

GETTING YOUR BEARINGS

Journeying through the Jurassic is no walk in the park. Sure, it's greener than the Triassic and more welcoming. There's fresh water and there are cool, shady forests to hang out in. But you'll have to share this space with far more creatures than during the Triassic, including dinosaurs of all shapes and sizes. And some of them are just not very good at sharing.

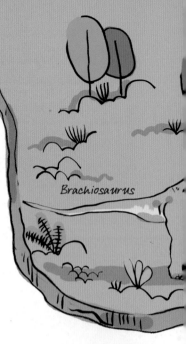

Brachiosaurus

Catch the drift?

Laurasia

Tethys Sea

Gondwana

With the start of the Jurassic, Pangaea has come to a parting of the ways. Titanic forces under Earth's crust have started ripping the supercontinent apart. Seawater is rushing into the cracks, forming new waterways and oceans. Two major continents are slowly shaping up: Laurasia in the north and Gondwana in the south, separated by a new stretch of ocean, the Tethys Sea.

Continents today

Jurassic continents

Make the most of those sunny spells

WEATHER EYE

You'll notice that it's still warm, but thankfully not as hot as during the Triassic. And those rain showers are really refreshing, aren't they? Trouble is, they seldom let up, and you could start to feel a little soggy after a while.

Light, waterproof, quick-drying clothes are what you need here.

Giraffatitan

The huge North American herbivore Brachiosaurus has an African relative called Giraffatitan.

Distant cousins

Once landmasses separate, dinosaurs that were originally the same species may develop in different ways. Toward the end of the Jurassic, there are already dinosaurs that are clearly from the same group but are now different enough to be considered separate species. Distant cousins, if you like!

Don't be a stick-in-the-mud—keep scanning the ground and choose a firm footing.

Durable hiking shoes or, even better, waterproof boots, will really prove their worth here.

Lie of the land

With the weather wetter and ocean levels rising, creeks are gurgling happily, rivers are flowing, lakes are filling. You'll be splashing through puddles and hopping over streams—and maybe finding yourself up to your waist in mud if you're not careful.

THE JURASSIC SCENE

With more water around, plants are thriving, sprouting thick foliage, seed cones, and even fruits. That means food galore for a huge range of plant-eating creatures. And where there are plant eaters aplenty, carnivores and scavengers will be making the most of it too. Everywhere you look, life is flourishing. It's getting busy!

WELL WATERED

You know how it works in your garden: water them well and your plants start sprouting. That's what's happening here. Trees are getting even taller, bushes bushier. Ferns are spreading over every patch of open ground. In places it's hard to fight your way through the foliage.

Ouch! the first blood-sucking insects have emerged. Cover up!

SHE MUST BE UNDER HERE SOMEWHERE!

A REAL BUZZ

Notice that buzzing sound? Insects are thriving. For some time flies and beetles have been playing a part in recycling decaying plants and flesh. Now insects are helping carry pollen between the first pollen-producing plants. Still no bees or butterflies though.

Plants called Bennettitaleans produce pollen to attract insects.

BENEATH THE WAVES

If the water is clear enough, you might be able to see coral and sponges, which are starting to form colonies. Deeper down, the first squidlike creatures are swimming around, being pursued by fishlike ichthyosaurs—big aquatic reptiles. Not that the ichthyosaurs can rest easy either, for even bigger monsters lurk in these seas. Swimming is not recommended!

Ichthyosaurs are usually 7-13 ft. (2-4 m) long. They feed on squid and fish.

Liopleurodon is the Jurassic's top underwater predator. Its jaws alone are as big as you!

SHORE THINGS

If you're a beachcomber, you'll enjoy the Jurassic. Scan the seashore and you'll find shells galore, including the distinctive spiral shells of ammonites.

In medieval times people thought that ammonites were fossilized snakes.

Mesolimulus looks like a modern-day horseshoe crab.

Pterodactylus

BETTER LUCK NEXT TIME!

Dakosaurus, the "biter lizard," is one of the largest crocodylomorphs, at up to 16 ft. (5 m) long.

Corals and sponges

Geosaurus is a crocodilian with a streamlined body, a fishlike tail, and flippers.

NEVER SMILE AT . . .

. . . a crocodylomorph. Here that's any member of the Jurassic crocodile family. If you think today's crocs are scary, check out these alarming ancestors—from a safe distance! During the Jurassic, crocs spend most or all of their time in the water, and many have developed paddle-like claws for swimming in the ocean.

FIELD GUIDE:
AT A STRETCH

THESE ARE THE BIGGEST LAND ANIMALS EVER!

Following another mass extinction near the end of the Triassic that wiped out most other large land reptiles, dinosaurs are now in full control on land. And with all of this food around, some are going through a growth spurt. That certainly makes them easy to spot!

Going up!

With trees growing taller and competition for food at ground level getting fiercer, some lizard-hipped plant eaters known as sauropods have decided that the only way is up. They're developing ever-longer necks to snack on leaves and branches that other dinosaurs just can't reach. Scan the treetops and you might see their small heads snaking through the greenery.

Mamenchisaurus has the longest neck of any dinosaur—up to 43 ft. (13 m).

Some large sauropods can live for up to 80 years!

The legs of sauropods are thick trunks of solid bone. But their upper bones contain holes and hollows to make them lighter.

Brachiosaurus has a shorter tail, longer front legs, and a more erect stance.

SAUROPOD SAFETY

When you're the size of a sauropod, there's simply no place to hide. So how do you protect yourself against predators?

Stand your ground: Your sheer size is a deterrent to most meat eaters.

THE INSECTS ARE BAD TODAY.

Stick together: One sauropod is imposing, but several together are all but unstoppable.

CHEESE!

Camarasaurus

Mamenchisaurus

IT'S OKAY, THEY DON'T BITE.

A sauropod's long neck can't support a heavy skull, so the head is usually small.

Barosaurus can rear up on its hind legs, allowing it to reach a height of 50 ft. (15 m).

Diplodocus is up to 98 ft. (30 m) long. Its neck alone can measure 21 ft. (6.4 m).

Camarasaurus is shorter and stockier and browses on lower branches.

Gastroliths

DOWN THE HATCH!

As you'll have noticed, the leaves on those trees are pretty tough. I bet you don't feel like dining out on them, do you? So how do these titanic herbivores cope with chewy plant matter? Edge close enough while they're eating and you might see that their teeth are shaped for cutting and tearing, but they have no grinding teeth like your molars. Mostly they don't chew, and they simply swallow leaves whole.

Rumbling belly?

So why don't sauropods get indigestion? Well, in their stomachs are round stones that the dinosaurs have deliberately swallowed. Shifting around in their bellies as they move, the stones—known as gastroliths— help mash up leaves and branches so that they can be digested.

Start swinging: One swipe of that tremendous tail should clear the way.

Pull out your secret weapon (if you've got one!): *Diplodocus* can crack its tail like a whip, creating a deafening sound that scares off attackers.

IF ONLY MY ARMS WERE LONGER, I COULD COVER MY EARS!

FIELD GUIDE:
ON GUARD

Not to be outdone, many bird-hipped plant eaters have become big guys too. Not only that, but they have developed their own weaponry to keep predators at bay. Herbivores they may be, but you don't want to get on their bad side!

> JUST STAY AWAY FROM THEIR TAILS!

Stegosaurus has tail triangular plates along its back and between four and eight tail spikes, each up to 3 ft. (1 m) long.

Prickly characters

As you'll see, *Stegosaurus* and other members of the stegosaur family are a little on the slow side—there's not much chance of them outrunning any predator. But their heads, backs, and tails are clad with thick skin, plates, and spurs to block bites and slashing claws. And with their spiked tails they can turn the tables on their attackers, impaling an opponent with one powerful swipe.

HIDING OUT

Understandably in this land of giants, small herbivores keep a low profile. They tend to stay hidden in the undergrowth, feeding on shrubs and ferns. To escape from predators, they rely on their speed and their ability to hide in tight spaces.

Kentrosaurus has up to seven pairs of spikes on its back and one long spike on each shoulder.

Tuojiangosaurus has up to 17 pairs of narrow, pointed plates on its back and four dagger-like spikes on its tail.

PLATE POWER?

The plates on the back of *Stegosaurus* might not just be for protection. They could have other purposes too. Here are some of the latest theories:

Blood flows through the plates, so by turning them to face the Sun, *Stegosaurus* can warm up. And by turning them in line with the Sun, it can cool down—useful in this cookin' climate!

The plates on every *Stegosaurus* are slightly different so that they can recognize one another.

HEY, IT'S SPOTS!

WHY IS HE SO POPULAR?

The plates are a way to show off. Particularly large or impressive ones help attract a mate.

Try observing *Stegosaurus* to find out what the plates are really for.

HEY, WHERE'D MY LUNCH GO?

Othnielosaurus has a beaklike jaw and powerful back legs for high-speed getaways.

Dryosaurus's strong back legs help it reach speeds of up to 25 mph (40 km/h).

FIELD GUIDE:
CRAFTY CARNIVORES

So, with their sheer bulk and all their nifty defenses, what do Jurassic plant eaters have to be afraid of? In a word: plenty. Dinosaur predators have not only edged out the competition among other reptiles, they've also started getting bigger, faster, and smarter. Everyone needs to be on their guard—and that includes you!

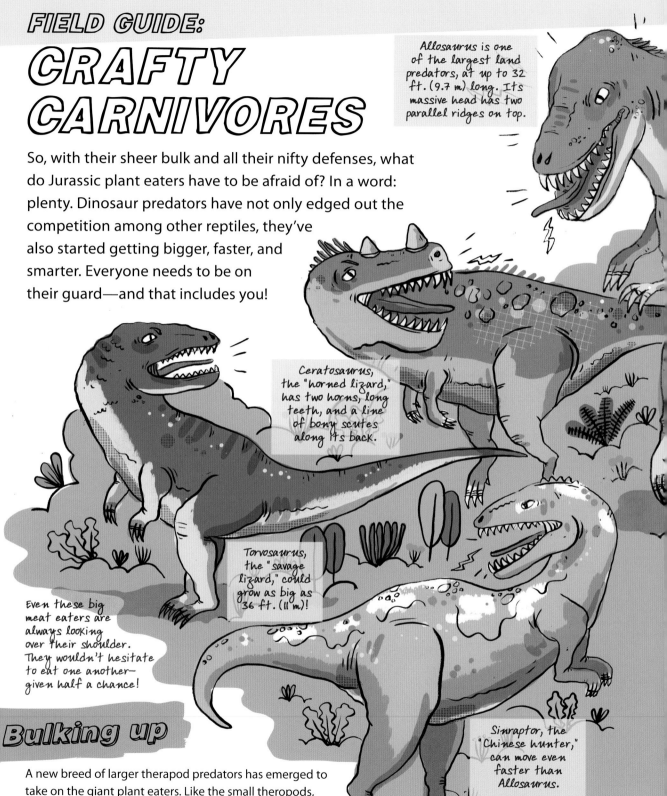

Allosaurus is one of the largest land predators, at up to 32 ft. (9.7 m) long. Its massive head has two parallel ridges on top.

Ceratosaurus, the "horned lizard," has two horns, long teeth, and a line of bony scutes along its back.

Torvosaurus, the "savage lizard," could grow as big as 36 ft. (11 m)!

Even these big meat eaters are always looking over their shoulder. They wouldn't hesitate to eat one another—given half a chance!

Sinraptor, the "Chinese hunter," can move even faster than Allosaurus.

Bulking up

A new breed of larger therapod predators has emerged to take on the giant plant eaters. Like the small theropods, they typically run on two legs, and they have a thick tail and small arms. But these giants can be as big as a bus and, most alarmingly, have a huge head, massive jaws, and rows of long, pointed teeth.

Archaeopteryx is considered the first bird.

Small strategists

Little hunters still abound, and they're coming up with some clever strategies too. Several small dinosaurs have developed feathers, for example, but *Archaeopteryx* is the first to take to the wing. Being able to fly even short distances gives it the edge over its rivals.

I JUST CAN'T GET THE HANG OF THIS!

Eosinopteryx was feathered but flightless.

Hatchet face

It's thought that carnivores such as *Allosaurus* could open their jaws especially wide and use their long teeth to slash large prey. Then they would simply wait for them to weaken from blood loss before moving in for the kill.

I THINK WE'VE BEEN SPOTTED!

SECURITY ALERT!

With carnivores getting bigger and craftier, it pays to be cautious:

- Stay downwind so that your scent doesn't drift their way.

- Don't carry food or leave any in the open at camp.

- Wear camouflage clothes to make you less conspicuous.

- Keep a low profile—don't do anything that draws attention.

TIME'S UP!

Actually, it looks like you're in a really tight corner here. And, with the blood now flowing, these carnivores are really on the rampage. It might be time to make a swift exit and make your way back to the safety of the 21st century!

It's the biggest theropod ever. And you thought that was *Tyrannosaurus!* See page 94.

✗ Ténéré

NIGER

Digging in the desert? Don't forget the deck chairs. Turn to page 96.

CONGO

One way to feed a whole tribe. See page 93.

Where did southern Africa's coolest dinosaurs hang out? See page 100.

The original big dead lizard? See page 101.

Karoo Basin ✗

• CAPE TOWN

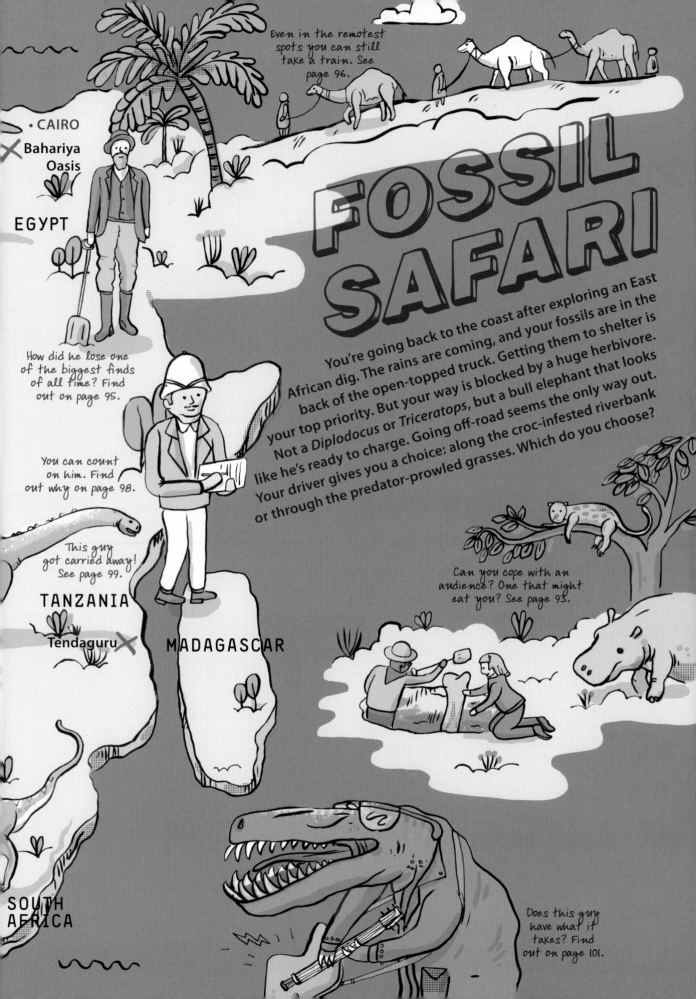

FOSSIL SAFARI

You're going back to the coast after exploring an East African dig. The rains are coming, and your fossils are in the back of the open-topped truck. Getting them to shelter is your top priority. But your way is blocked by a huge herbivore. Not a Diplodocus or Triceratops, but a bull elephant that looks like he's ready to charge. Going off-road seems the only way out. Your driver gives you a choice: along the croc-infested riverbank or through the predator-prowled grasses. Which do you choose?

Even in the remotest spots you can still take a train. See page 96.

CAIRO

Bahariya Oasis

EGYPT

How did he lose one of the biggest finds of all time? Find out on page 95.

You can count on him. Find out why on page 98.

This guy got carried away! See page 99.

TANZANIA

Tendaguru

MADAGASCAR

Can you cope with an audience? One that might eat you? See page 93.

SOUTH AFRICA

Does this guy have what it takes? Find out on page 101.

HUNTER'S QUEST

Traveling in Africa can be trying. Just getting to fossil sites might involve epic treks through sweat-spilling jungle, scorching desert, and grasslands prowled by terrifying predators. And you might have to deal with extreme weather, deadly diseases, maybe even a war zone or two. Are you tough enough to tackle it?

A lively place

MUST BE SOME WEIRD HUMAN DANCE.

One week you might be scouring for Late Cretaceous specimens in the Sahara Desert, one of the driest, hottest places in the world, where there's hardly a drop of water to drink and barely a sign of life. The next you might be hacking your way through Central African jungle where absolutely everything seems alive—including your underwear!

NOW I REALLY HAVE ANTS IN MY PANTS!

DIG DEEPER

• •

IZIKO SOUTH AFRICAN MUSEUM

Africa is so big that it can be hard to know where to start. To get your bearings, check out the Iziko South African Museum in Cape Town. Its African Dinosaurs exhibit displays dozens of fossils collected from all over the continent and provides helpful information on the major sites. As you'll see, fossils from all periods have been found here, but there's little from the Mid-Jurassic. Can you help plug that gap?

Being watched

The slightly milder, more open grasslands of East Africa could provide some relief. But while you're digging up a long-dead carnivore, there could be some livelier present-day ones eyeing you up for lunch. Can you keep digging—and keep your nerve?

OLD TIMER

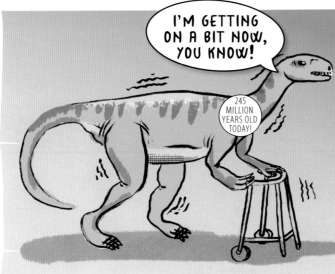

It took more than half a century to figure it out, but a dinosaur found in East Africa may be the oldest yet discovered. Found in Tanzania in 1956, *Nyasasaurus* was not fully described and dated until 2013. The results suggest that it lived 245 million years ago— about 15 million years earlier than what had been considered the earliest dinosaur, South America's *Eoraptor*.

Forest lore

Travel deep into the jungles of the Congo in West Africa and you might help solve one of the great dinosaur-related mysteries of the continent. Native people have long told of a sauropod-like creature that dwells in and around the waters of Lake Tele, known as Mokele-mbembe. Since the 1700s there have been dozens of sightings of it, and in the past 50 years more than 20 expeditions have been mounted to search for it.

In 1959 a group of Pygmies claimed to have killed and eaten a Mokele-mbembe. Must have been quite a snack!

LOST IN THE DESERT

Spanning much of North Africa, the Sahara is today the hottest and largest of the world's deserts. But beneath its endless stony plains and rolling seas of sand lie the fossilized remains of Mesozoic lands that once teemed with life.

Wrong size

Sometimes you find amazing things when you aren't even looking for them. German scientist Ernst Stromer started sifting the Saharan sands in 1910, searching for the remains of early humans and other mammals. A year later, at Bahariya Oasis (southwest of Cairo, Egypt), he came upon a clutch of far bigger finds: fossilized bones of Late Cretaceous dinosaurs.

NO, THAT'S NOT IT . . . NO, WRONG AGAIN.

Daytime temperatures in the Sahara can reach 122°F (50°C).

The sail may have been used to scare predators, attract mates, or control body temperature.

WE'LL ALL BE EXTINCT BY THE TIME THIS SHIP SAILS!

SAIL? I'LL SHOW YOU A SAIL!

Cretaceous cargo

Stuck in port

The fossils were so huge that Stromer had trouble transporting them. Eventually he arranged for them to be shipped to Germany. But then World War I broke out and the delivery was delayed—for 11 years! When the bones finally arrived, they were in such bad shape that it took Stromer another nine years to piece them back together.

Fortunately it was worth the wait. Stromer's Cretaceous cargo consisted of fossils of four carnivorous theropod dinosaurs, including the biggest predator ever to walk the planet, *Spinosaurus*. As long as two city buses and with its long, fang-filled jaws, strong, three-clawed hands, and huge sail, it outdid even *Tyrannosaurus* in the terror stakes.

BOMBED OUT

Stromer might have had it tough during World War I, but it was nothing compared with what was in store for him in World War II. On April 24, 1944, during a British air raid on Munich, Germany, a bomb landed on the city museum, obliterating every one of his fossils. All he had left were his notes.

I'M SO GLAD THEY CAME BACK FOR ME!

Back to the start

To make matters worse, Stromer never mapped his finds. So when later paleontologists decided to search for the site, they had only his notes to go on. But eventually they found not only his site but also further fossils of his famous finds, plus some new ones, including the arm bone of one of the biggest sauropods ever unearthed. In 2001 it was named *Paratitlan stromeri*, "Stromer's tidal giant."

Paratitlan

Spinosaurus used its crocodilian jaw to snap up huge fish from shallow waters.

I FINALLY GOT MY JUST DESERT!

EYE, EYE!

Recently another North African predator was identified by paleontologists, based on a single piece of bone from the eye socket of a skull. The eye reminded the scientists of the Eye of Sauron in *The Lord of the Rings*, so they gave it that name in Latin: *Sauroniops*.

RIVERS BENEATH THE SAND

Now that you've learned to deal with the desert, you'll be ready to tackle one of the most challenging fossil sites in the Sahara. In the Ténéré region of northern Niger, dinosaur bones literally litter the sands. But the region is so remote, waterless, and hot that hardly anyone goes there—let alone digs there!

Wind work

It's hard to believe today, but for much of the Mesozoic the Ténéré was a green, swampy region traversed by swift-flowing rivers. Many dinosaur remains were washed into the waterways, formed fossils underground, and have since been exposed by shifting sands. At some spots you don't even have to dig—the wind does the work for you!

> CAN YOU IDENTIFY IT FROM HERE, OR DO WE HAVE TO GET UP?

Dinosaur vertebrae

Super Croc!

Sarcosuchus was twice the length of any modern croc.

The skull is as long as an adult human!

In the 1960s a team of French paleontologists discovered a spectacular skull of an Early Cretaceous crocodile-like reptile in the Ténéré and named it *Sarcosuchus imperator*. When US dinosaur hunter Paul Sereno found similar bones in the 1990s, the creature quickly became known as Super Croc—and for good reason!

Sarcosuchus was as long and almost as heavy as a city bus. Like to climb aboard?

Desert style

The Ténéré is a vast sea of sand covering 150,000 sq. mi. (400,000 sq km). The native Tuareg people have learned to cope with the harsh conditions here and use camels to carry goods across the desert. You can learn a lot from the Tuareg. Their loose-fitting robes help keep them cool, while the men's wraparound head scarf, or Tagelmust, protects their faces during sandstorms.

Other species you might trip over here include the sail-backed herbivore *Ouranosaurus* and the Jurassic predator *Afrovenator*.

Tuareg driver

In the Sahara, sand can pile up in dunes as big as small mountains—up to 1,526 ft. (465 m) high!

If you're really smart, you'll get someone to do your driving too—preferably a local!

A toothy grin

Sereno found other bizarre bones too, such as this skull. It looks like an attachment for a vacuum cleaner, doesn't it? But it is in fact the skull of *Nigersaurus*, an Early Cretaceous herbivore. The front of the oddly shaped jaw was lined with more than 50 teeth, behind each of which were rows of replacements. That meant a mouthful of around 500 teeth in all!

Nigersaurus moved its head over the ground, snipping plants—more like a lawn mower than a vacuum cleaner!

With its eyes on the ground, Nigersaurus may not have noticed Sarcosuchus—until it was too late!

THE LONG HAUL

If you find a bumper crop of bones, your first thought will be, "Yeah!" And your second might be, "Uh-oh, how the heck do I get this home?" Today the answer could be trucks or helicopters, but in early 20th-century East Africa the only solution was hundreds of pairs of helping hands—and feet.

Tendaguru is the only place in the world where Kentrosaurus bones have been found. More than 1,200 were unearthed.

A well-worn path

When German fossil hunters found Late Jurassic bones at Tendaguru in Tanzania in 1907, they organized the biggest dinosaur-hunting expedition ever to bring it all home. The site was only 40 mi. (65 km) from the port of Lindi, but in those days there were no railroads or roads through the tropical forest. The solution was to hire hundreds of African porters to make the four-day hike. In the end it took them four years to get all of the fossils out!

Kentrosaurus

I'VE ALREADY RUN OUT OF FINGERS!

DOING THE NUMBERS

For the first three years the expedition was headed by paleontologist Werner Janensch. He hired more than 1,000 local workers, many of whom brought their families along with them. That meant all of their supplies had to be carried in from the coast too. Keeping track of it all was a major headache!

Predators included Allosaurus and Ceratosaurus, both of which had previously been found in North America, as well as Elaphrosaurus, a fast-moving theropod up to 20 ft. (6 m) long.

Between 1909 and 1911, the porters:
* made 5,400 journeys
* transported 4,300 loads of bones
* packed 800 crates with fossils weighing 200 tons (185 tonnes)

THIS WAY UP

AND THEY THINK MONKEYS ARE NUTS?!

DON'T YOU DARE TICKLE MY TOES!

Another large sauropod was named *Janenschia* in honor of Janensch. It was more than 80 ft. (24 m) long and weighed at least 33 tons (30 tonnes).

HEY, ISN'T THAT MY LEG BACK THERE?

HIGH RISE

Almost 100 complete skeletons were shipped to Germany, though it took years to reassemble some of them. The largest was a *Brachiosaurus* skeleton that now dominates the collection of Berlin's Natural History Museum. Four stories high, it's still the tallest dinosaur skeleton ever mounted.

The biggest, heaviest bones belonged to a sauropod that Janensch identified as *Brachiosaurus*. It was later reclassified as *Giraffatitan*, an African relative of *Brachiosaurus*.

OFF-LIMITS

After World War I, the British took over the Tendaguru digs. But many expedition members became sick, and the party's leader, Canadian William E. Cutler, died of malaria. No major digs have taken place here since. Could you get things going again?

SOUTHERN STOREHOUSES

You'd better have plenty of energy, because you've got a lot of ground to cover in the south. The Karoo Basin is a gold mine of early dinosaur fossils, but they are scattered across a vast area spanning two thirds of South Africa. And if you plan to investigate the fossils of Madagascar (off the east coast), you'll have to travel the length of the world's fourth-largest island. Whew!

Desert slab

The Karoo Basin is one gargantuan slab of sedimentary rocks laid down between the Permian and Jurassic periods. During the Late Triassic and Early Jurassic, it was a huge expanse of desert with sparse plant life.

LESOTHOSAURUS

Smaller dog-size herbivores such as *Lesothosaurus* scurried around in groups, nibbling on plants and snapping up insects.

Long, slim legs for fast running

Heterodontosaurus had five fingers and may have been able to use them to grasp plants.

CHECK 'EM OUT!

Can't find shade in the desert? You can always make your own. That's what small herbivores like *Lesothosaurus* and *Heterodontosaurus* did. They dug underground burrows in which to sit out the hottest times of the day or year.

COOL PAD, MAN!

TRUTH OF THE TEETH?

Most dinosaurs made do with one kind of tooth, but *Heterodontosaurus* had three. At the front were sharp teeth for chopping plants. At the back were bigger teeth for grinding them up. Between were tusklike teeth that are a bit of a puzzle. Were they used for ripping up roots, tearing meat, or just showing off to rivals? Can you figure it out?

MASSOSPONDYLUS

Massospondylus was an early cousin of the Jurassic sauropods, but smaller and leaner. When plants were in short supply, it may have eaten small creatures, too.

MEGAPNOSAURUS

Herbivores had to keep watch for roving bands of *Megapnosaurus*, an early theropod predator. About 10 ft. (3 m) in length, it had a long snout and short, sharp teeth.

Distinctive nasal crests

The name *Megapnosaurus* sounds impressive, doesn't it? But it simply means "big dead lizard"!

Out on a limb

You might expect fossils found in Madagascar, off the southeast coast of Africa, to be just more of the same. But the island has many unique fossils, and some have links to other parts of the world.

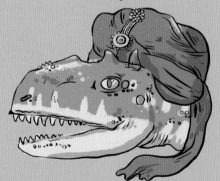

THE INDIAN CONNECTION

After the southern continent of Gondwana broke up 135 million years ago, India remained attached to Madagascar for another 50 million years or so. As a result, many of Madagascar's Late Cretaceous dinosaurs have Indian connections, including the predator *Majungasaurus*, which is related to the Indian dinosaurs *Rajasaurus* and *Indosaurus*.

ROCK STAR

In 2001 a US team found a Late Cretaceous predator with front teeth that stuck out from its jaw at a weird angle, probably to help it snatch up prey. They gave it the full name of *Masiakasaurus knopfleri*, after Mark Knopfler, leader of the rock band Dire Straits—not because he has weird teeth but because they liked to listen to his music as they worked.

Which giant has you in its clutches? Find out on page 111.

RUSSIA

What a fearful set of gnashers! Find out who they belong to on page 110.

Fancy feathers are on show across eastern Asia. Learn more on page 105.

MONGOLIA

Nemegt Basin ✗   ✗ Flaming Cliffs

Is this guy for real? Find out on page 104.

This dino has a sting in its tail. See page 113.

BEIJING

Dashanpu

CHINA

INDIA

This museum's prize exhibit is an entire quarry. See page 113.

Young he may be, but he's the grand old man of Chinese paleontology. Turn to page 107.

The things that myths are made of? See page 106.

Liaoning

REALM OF THE DRAGON

In a mountain village on the Chinese flank of Asia's Gobi Desert, the locals try to warn you away. It's the lair of a great winged monster, they say. No way should you go there. They show you rocks found by some of their more intrepid neighbors, which they say have special powers. But you forge on and find the cave and, sure enough, its walls are studded with fossils. It's a thrilling discovery. But hold on, what's that rumbling from the depths of the tunnel? And why are your guides all charging for the exit?

Grate for a huge headache. Directions on page 106.

He raced ahead in Mongolia. Learn more on page 108.

HUNTER'S QUEST

Make sure you have plenty of room in your cases. Because, after a slow start, Asia has become the dinosaur hunter's happiest hunting ground—more dinosaurs have now been found here than on any other continent.

Changing scene

You'll have every hope of striking it lucky in China and Mongolia. And in fast-developing eastern China, you can hole up in hotels and zip around on some of the world's speediest trains. Out west, though, it's another story. Home comforts are few and far between. Plus, from central China some of the world's most extreme deserts stretch north across Mongolia and west toward Europe.

THAT'S NO DINOSAUR!

In the spring, winds whip up huge sandstorms in western China that can spread across the country.

BRAND-NEW SPECIES: MADEUPOSAURUS.

BLACK MARKET

Psst! Wanna buy a dinosaur skeleton? Maybe not. Fossil smuggling, or dinosaur rustling, as it's also known, is common in China and Mongolia. And many fossils may not be quite what they seem. In 2012 the skeleton of a *Tarbosaurus*, a *Tyrannosaurus*-like predator, was sent from Mongolia and sold at auction in New York for US$1 million. Closer investigation showed that it had been pieced together using bones from several different species!

No, really!

Fakes aside, some of the most unlikely-looking dinosaurs from Asia are real. Which would be your pick in this parade of the continent's kookiest creatures?

INCISIVOSAURUS

Part of the fashionable feathered crowd from Early Cretaceous China, *Incisivosaurus* has gorgeous feathers and a winning smile. *Incisivosaurus*'s ambition is to learn how to fly.

Woolly wonders

Further north, dinosaur fossils are a bit thin on the frequently frozen ground of eastern Russia, or Siberia. But the region is famous for fabulously preserved fossils of giants of another era—the woolly mammoths of the Late Quaternary Period (500,000 to 100,000 years ago). Sadly for them, mammoths had the misfortune to be around at the same time as a group of fiendish predators that probably helped wipe them out: humans.

The biggest mammoths were around 16.5 ft. (5 m) tall, covered in thick hair, and had gigantic, curved tusks.

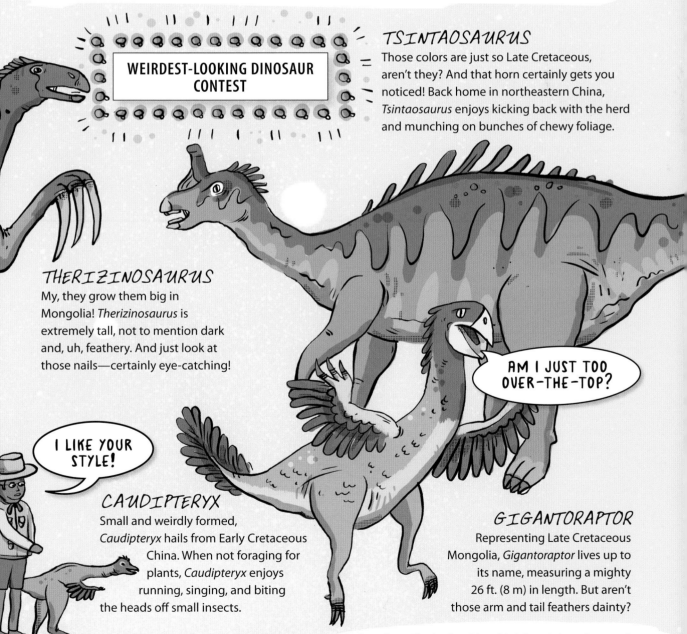

WEIRDEST-LOOKING DINOSAUR CONTEST

TSINTAOSAURUS

Those colors are just so Late Cretaceous, aren't they? And that horn certainly gets you noticed! Back home in northeastern China, *Tsintaosaurus* enjoys kicking back with the herd and munching on bunches of chewy foliage.

THERIZINOSAURUS

My, they grow them big in Mongolia! *Therizinosaurus* is extremely tall, not to mention dark and, uh, feathery. And just look at those nails—certainly eye-catching!

AM I JUST TOO OVER-THE-TOP?

I LIKE YOUR STYLE!

CAUDIPTERYX

Small and weirdly formed, *Caudipteryx* hails from Early Cretaceous China. When not foraging for plants, *Caudipteryx* enjoys running, singing, and biting the heads off small insects.

GIGANTORAPTOR

Representing Late Cretaceous Mongolia, *Gigantoraptor* lives up to its name, measuring a mighty 26 ft. (8 m) in length. But aren't those arm and tail feathers dainty?

So, who will win the title of Asia's weirdest dinosaur?

BEYOND THE MYTHS

As far as we know, no dinosaur ever breathed fire. But dinosaurs could be the source of many Eastern myths about the large, scaly, reptilian beasts that we call dragons.

Early records

Descriptions of dragon bones in Chinese texts dating from the AD 200s may be the world's oldest records of dinosaur fossils. It's thought now that what were referred to as dragon bones were probably the remains of prehistoric reptiles, including Jurassic sauropods and pterosaurs—which may have given rise to the idea of dragon wings.

Just the tonic!

Got any aches and pains? Feeling a little woozy? Maybe a little dinosaur bone will help. In China dragons are seen as protective beings, so anything that comes from a dragon is thought to keep you from harm. For centuries people have been grinding up so-called dragon bones for medicinal uses.

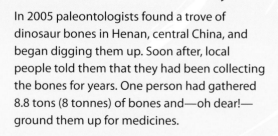

TAKE TWO A DAY.

In 2005 paleontologists found a trove of dinosaur bones in Henan, central China, and began digging them up. Soon after, local people told them that they had been collecting the bones for years. One person had gathered 8.8 tons (8 tonnes) of bones and—oh dear!—ground them up for medicines.

FOREIGN AID

International teams of fossil hunters began foraging in Asia in the early 1900s. A Russian team made an early visit to China in 1915. In the late 1920s Swedish scientists helped Chinese teams find the country's first new dinosaur species, *Euhelopus*, an early sauropod measuring up to 49 ft. (15 m) in length.

> FOLLOW ME TO PAGE 108!

Leading the pack deeper into Asia was a major expedition from the American Museum of Natural History, headed by adventurer Roy Chapman Andrews.

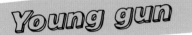

Young gun

Chinese dinosaur hunters began to get more organized during the 1930s, under the leadership of Yang Zhongjian, or as he was known in the West, C. C. Young. One of his earliest discoveries was an Early Jurassic herbivore, *Lufengosaurus*. In 1958 it became the first dinosaur skeleton to be mounted in China.

> NOW I'LL REALLY GET TO TRAVEL!

To commemorate the discovery of *Lufengosaurus*, a special set of postage stamps was issued—the first time a dinosaur had ever made it onto a stamp!

DIG DEEPER

• •

THE IVPP, BEIJING

C. C. Young was the driving force behind the creation of China's Institute of Vertebrate Paleontology and Paleoanthropology. (That's kind of a mouthful, so people usually just call it the IVPP.) It houses many of Asia's most important fossils and is a great place to start your Asian odyssey. The IVPP has more than 200,000 specimens, and its displays include a magnificent skeleton of *Lufengosaurus*.

C. C. Young was China's leading dinosaur expert for over 40 years.

Lufengosaurus

A HOT SPOT

When Roy Chapman Andrews drove his team into the Mongolian desert in 1922 and found the Cretaceous site that they named the Flaming Cliffs, they had to deal with searing heat, intense cold, sandstorms, marauding bandits, a lack of water, and cars getting repeatedly stuck in the sand. Today you should have an easier time—but don't count on it!

Off-road

Andrews's team rode in from Beijing in a convoy of Dodge cars. Time and again they got stuck in deep sand, blew out tires, or even crashed into rocks.

As well as five touring cars, the expedition included 125 camels, 2 trucks, and 40 people.

ARE YOU SURE IT'S WORKING?

A PLACE OF EXTREMES

Even now, the Gobi Desert is a fearsome place. There are hardly any roads or settlements, water is hard to find, and temperatures are extreme. Going into a desert, you'd be prepared for heat, but in the Gobi you may have to deal with the opposite problem too. The mercury can soar to 104°F (40°C) in the summer and plummet to –40°F (–40°C) in the winter. Even in one day you can go from sweltering in the Sun to freezing at night.

Fight to the death

Andrews and his team returned in 1923 and 1925, but in 1930, following civil unrest, Mongolia was closed to Westerners—for the next 60 years! Eastern European and Russian expeditions were allowed in, however, and in 1971 a Polish-Mongolian team, led by Zofia Kielan-Jaworowska, made an amazing discovery: the skeletons of two dinosaurs, *Velociraptor* and *Protoceratops*, locked in mortal combat.

Protoceratops had clamped its stout, hooked beak onto Velociraptor's right arm.

Velociraptor, a small, fierce predator, was using its large hind claws to gouge at Protoceratops's neck.

Productive pit stop

Andrews was actually on the hunt for early human fossils. But during an unplanned pit stop, a chance discovery changed everything. Photographer J. B. Shackleford wandered off to look at some rock formations, stumbled, and almost went headfirst into a shallow canyon studded with dinosaur bones.

Among the finds in the canyon were fossilized eggs—the first anyone had found since Jean-Jacques Pouech in 1859 (see page 35).

As the two dinosaurs fought, a dune collapsed on top of them and killed them both.

REALITY CHECK

Thanks to the movie *Jurassic Park*, *Velociraptor* has become one of the most famous dinosaurs. But did the movie give us the right idea? Not quite.

IMPOSTOR!

MOVIE
* 6.6 ft. (2 m) high
* Scaly skin, no hair or feathers
* Fiendishly clever
* Dug up in Montana

REALITY
* 1.6 ft. (0.5 m) high
* Covered in feathers
* About as smart as a chicken
* Found only in Mongolia

Some of the differences were the result of confusion between *Velociraptor* and the similar but larger species *Deinonychus*. And, to be fair to the moviemakers, it wasn't until a few years after the movie was made that paleontologists realized *Velociraptor* had feathers.

FEARFUL FINDS

After the grueling conditions at Flaming Cliffs, you might be eager to get back to civilization. But it's worth hanging in there and taking a short detour south to the Nemegt Basin, for this site is said to be the richest source of Late Cretaceous dinosaurs in the world.

Scourge of Asia?

Tarbosaurus was as big as its relative, Tyrannosaurus, and had the same huge head, powerful jaws, and long, serrated teeth.

Did *Tyrannosaurus* have an equally terrifying Asian cousin? That's the thought that struck Russian and Mongolian dinosaur hunters when they came across a giant theropod skull in the Nemegt Basin in the late 1940s. Confirming that it was indeed a relative, they called it *Tyrannosaurus bataar* (*bataar* meaning "hero") and then changed the name to *Tarbosaurus*, from a Greek phrase meaning "terror lizard." Either way, it sends a shiver down your spine!

Speed stars

What do you need to be a fast runner? Long, powerful legs? A streamlined body? *Gallimimus*, an ostrich-like dinosaur dug up in the Nemegt Basin in the 1960s, seems to have had all of these qualities. And paleontologists have since calculated that it could have been one of the fastest dinosaurs of all time. So how do the others—and you—compare? Who'd win the Dinosaur Sprint?

AND THEY'RE OFF!

Velociraptor Highly favored, this light, nimble predator has no trouble zipping along at 25 mph (40 km/h).

Stegosaurus Not surprisingly, it's a lumbering start from this bulky beast, which can seldom move at more than 4–5 mph (6–8 km/h).

Human In lane two, our young human has started well and is topping 9 mph (15 km/h). Once he's an adult he might reach 19 mph (30 km/h).

Tyrannosaurus This guy gets everyone moving! Over a short distance *T. rex* can hit 19 mph (30 km/h), but the big predator is likely to tire quickly.

Diplodocus That giant stride lets *Diplodocus* cruise at about 9 mph (15 km/h). And if it gets wind of a predator, it could double that!

Terrible claws?

WE'RE BOTH GETTING A BIG HAND!

Come on, admit it. If you saw these claws reaching out for you, you'd be scared out of your wits, wouldn't you? The Polish team that found them in the Nemegt Basin in 1970 felt much the same and called the new species *Deinocheirus*, meaning "terrible or horrible hand." Yikes!

Gallimimus Pulling away is *Gallimimus*, already reaching a cruising speed of 40 mph (65 km/h). Is he home free?

Struthiomimus No, wait! Streaking down the outside lane at the amazing pace of 50 mph (80 km/h) is *Struthiomimus*, a Late Cretaceous ostrich dinosaur. Gold to *Struthiomimus*!

THAT'S HANDY!

Recent research suggests that *Deinocheirus* might not have been such a terror after all, but a placid—albeit giant—herbivore. Which just goes to show: you can't always judge a dinosaur by its claws.

DEINOCHEIRUS

It now appears that *Deinocheirus* was an ostrich-like dinosaur and used its huge claws mainly to gather leaves from high trees.

THERIZINOSAURUS

You might imagine these—the biggest claws of any animal ever, at 3 ft. (1 m)—raking through flesh. But *Therizinosaurus* was a herbivore and used its claws to reach high branches.

MONONYKUS

You'll need to look closely to see this little feathered theropod's claws. Each is just one long pointed spike. Perfect for poking pesky predators in the eye, of course. But paleontologists believe that their main use was for drilling into termite mounds to get to insects.

JURASSIC BONANZA

Few places offer a finer range of Mid-Jurassic fossils than Dashanpu in Sichuan, central China. And those fossils might all have been blasted, buried, and lost forever if it hadn't been for the determination of China's top dinosaur detective.

Gas works

In the early 1970s a Chinese gas company was excavating the area to create a storage depot. After blasting apart some rocks, workers found that they contained fragments of bones. These turned out to be from a small Mid-Jurassic carnivore. In honor of its finding place, it was later named *Gasosaurus constructus*.

Gasosaurus

Race against time

The discoveries drew the attention of Dong Zhiming, a former student of C. C. Young and at the time a rising star of Chinese paleontology. His investigations at the site in 1979 revealed hundreds, then thousands, of bones. Dong quickly persuaded the government to halt the gas depot construction and preserve the site as a fossil dig.

Dong and his team eventually unearthed more than 8,000 fossils and named 100 new dinosaurs from the site.

Dong has named more dinosaur species than any other living paleontologist. That's my boy!

A gathering place

So how did these dinosaurs end up hanging out in a dusty construction site? Well, it's thought that in the Mid-Jurassic, Sichuan was a land of forests and rushing rivers and that Dashanpu was the site of a lake. When dinosaurs died, the rivers may have carried their bones to the lake. Or a flash flood may have drowned many at one time.

Omeisaurus had the second-longest neck of any dinosaur.

The spiked tail of Shunosaurus was a highly effective weapon.

THAT'LL TEACH HIM!

Xiaosaurus was a small herbivore.

Gasosaurus hunted in packs.

Back off!

You know what they say: practice makes perfect. A group of paleontology students practicing their digging skills at a roadcut near Dashanpu turned up an entirely new species of Mid-Jurassic sauropod. And one with a difference. *Shunosaurus* had the long neck and tail typical of sauropods, but it also had an extra feature at the end of its tail: a spiked club that it used to whack predators.

DIG DEEPER

•••••••••••••••••••••••••••

ZIGONG DINOSAUR PARK

To help protect the Dashanpu discoveries, a new dinosaur museum was built. Huge openings in the floor of the museum allow visitors to view many bones still in place in the rocks and watch the park's paleontologists at work. Gigantic skeletons on display include those of *Omeisaurus*, *Shunosaurus*, and *Gasosaurus*.

OF A FEATHER?

In the mid-1990s a series of finds in Liaoning Province in northeastern China really set dinosaur hunters' hearts aflutter. Dozens of finely detailed fossils revealed that feathers and wings were far more common than previously thought—and not just among prehistoric birds.

Star of the show

In 1996 farmer Li Yinfang found a stone slab imprinted with the shape of a small reptile. It turned out to be one of the most momentous fossil finds of modern times. When scientists studied it, they saw that the reptile was a small theropod, but also that it had been covered in little, downy feathers. *Sinosauropteryx*, as it was named, was the first dinosaur—as opposed to a prehistoric bird—to be found with feathers. The discovery caused a sensation.

I NEVER DREAMED I'D BECOME SO FAMOUS!

Sinosauropteryx

Crow-sized *Confuciusornis* could fly well.

Flocking together

Further excavations revealed feathered creatures of all kinds. Some were prehistoric birds and were evolving toward flight. Others were dinosaurs, mostly small theropods like *Sinosauropteryx*. Their feathers kept them warm and may have helped attract a mate.

Microraptor could glide for short distances.

Scansoriopteryx used its hooked claws to scale trees.

Sinornithosaurus was a clumsy flier.

Caudipteryx strutted around on the ground.

THESE FEATHERS ARE HOPELESS!

Fine detail

The feathers in the Liaoning fossils are so clearly visible because of the substance in which the dinosaurs were buried. As these creatures died, volcanic eruptions spewed ash into the air. And when this ash set hard around the dinosaur remains, it preserved even the finest details.

I'M NOT READY TO BE A FOSSIL!

Any combination?

After seeing some of the Liaoning fossils, you'd almost believe in any combination of bones, feathers, scales, and fangs. So when a fossil turned up in the United States from Liaoning in 1999, people were ready to accept it as a new species, *Archaeoraptor*. But this fluffy flier turned out to be a fake: a fossil of a bird joined to a fossil of a dinosaur tail. No doubt there were a lot of red faces.

ALMOST FOOLED YOU!

Yutyrannus is the biggest feathered creature ever found —far too big for takeoff!

THE LONG AND THE SHORT OF IT

In northeastern China in the late 1970s, Dong Zhiming found a dinosaur that was among the smallest known, at barely 3 ft. (1 m) in length. Yet the name that he gave it is the longest of any dinosaur: *Micropachycephalosaurus hongtuyanensis*. Try saying that quickly! It means "small, thick-headed lizard."

MICROPACHYCEPHALOSAURUS HONGTUYANENSIS

It's the most titanic pterosaur of all! Find out more on page 121.

TIME TRIP: CRETACEOUS

Soon after landing in the Late Cretaceous, 65 million years back in time, you go on your craziest adventure yet: tracking a Tyrannosaurus. Following its prints into the trees, you hear a sickening crunching noise and a low growl. In a clearing, the nightmarish beast is bent over a young Edmontosaurus, ripping at its flanks with fearsome fangs. As you take a closer look, the branch that you're leaning on snaps. The monstrous carnivore turns. Will you be dessert? You freeze, petrified . . . But then the Tyrannosaurus resumes its gory meal. You slowly back off. That's close enough!

Hear those sounds? What are they saying? And how? Turn to page 123.

GETTING YOUR BEARINGS

Experience of the Triassic and Jurassic will prepare you well for the Cretaceous. You are in for a few surprises, though, and will need all your survival skills to stay safe.

Catch the drift?

The continents are really cracking up now, and by the Late Cretaceous they have more or less taken up the positions they have in our time. But sea levels are rising too, so water is rushing into every crack and spreading across low-lying land. North America and North Africa are both split down the middle by seas. Europe and Asia are clusters of large islands.

Land during Late Cretaceous   Continents today

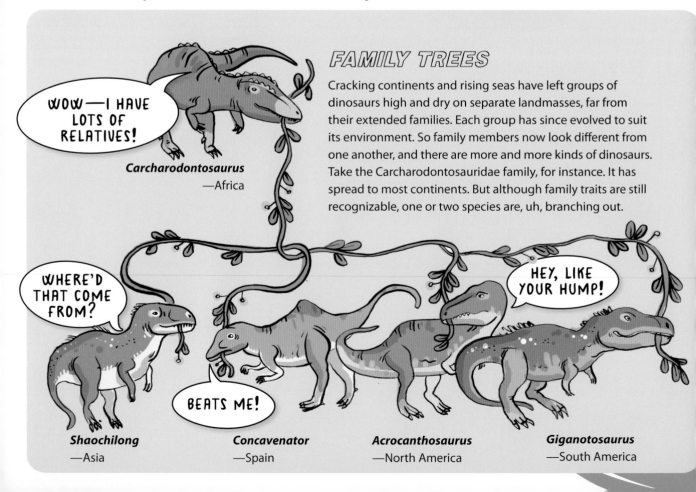

FAMILY TREES

Cracking continents and rising seas have left groups of dinosaurs high and dry on separate landmasses, far from their extended families. Each group has since evolved to suit its environment. So family members now look different from one another, and there are more and more kinds of dinosaurs. Take the Carcharodontosauridae family, for instance. It has spread to most continents. But although family traits are still recognizable, one or two species are, uh, branching out.

WOW—I HAVE LOTS OF RELATIVES!

Carcharodontosaurus
—Africa

WHERE'D THAT COME FROM?

BEATS ME!

HEY, LIKE YOUR HUMP!

Shaochilong
—Asia

Concavenator
—Spain

Acrocanthosaurus
—North America

Giganotosaurus
—South America

WEATHER EYE

It's so hard to pack for the Cretaceous! The weather varies more from place to place and is far more changeable than in the Jurassic. Summers are getting hotter, winters colder. Ice sheets are spreading around the South Pole. You don't quite know what you'll be in for—so it's best to have it all covered.

Cool headgear for a cold snap

Wet suits are fab for those flooded areas.

Volcanic activity is on the rise.

Lie of the land

In the millions of years that have passed since the Triassic, earth movements, wind, and water have had time to work the land into weird and wonderful shapes. Major mountain ranges have sprung up, including North America's Rocky Mountains and Europe's Alps. Forests cover much of the land, but jagged peaks jut above the trees.

OR THE BEGINNING OF THE END?

COULD THIS BE THE START OF SOMETHING?

THE CRETACEOUS SCENE

You might think not much has changed since the Jurassic. The forests are still mainly conifers, and you're still swishing through ferns at almost every step. But one difference should catch your eye right away: flowers. The world is in bloom, and brilliant new colors are everywhere!

Bloomin' lovely

Check out those magnificent blooms up in that magnolia tree. And how about those pink water lilies at the edge of that pond? What a difference they make to this world!

New forms of insects have evolved to help out with pollination, including the first bees and butterflies.

Magnolia

Sequoia tree—In our age, these are the biggest trees on Earth.

GOING NUTS

Nut-bearing trees such as hazels, walnuts, and oaks grow in some areas, providing new kinds of food.

Water lilies

FED UP?

Insects? Seeds? Nuts? Nectar? It all sounds mouthwatering to small mammals. No surprise, then, that their numbers are on the rise. And among them are growing numbers of marsupials—mammals that carry their young in pouches.

Alphadon, a marsupial

Giant of the air

Insects and birds are competing for air space with flying reptiles. And some of those reptiles take up a lot of space! *Quetzalcoatlus* is a gargantuan pterosaur measuring a whopping 39 ft. (12 m) from wing tip to wing tip—that's wider than some jet fighters today!

The really bad news is that Quetzalcoatlus is a carnivore and regularly stalks and kills small dinosaurs—or anything of a similar size. Be on your guard!

Ichthyornis looks and flies a little like a big seagull. Its little jagged teeth are perfect for hanging on to slippery fish.

Winging it

From the first few feathered species, all sorts of birds have evolved, in all parts of the world. Some feast on flowers, seeds, and nectar, while others dive underwater to catch fish.

Hesperornis, a wingless waterbird, looks streamlined as it dives for fish. But on land it has to slither on its stomach like a penguin.

Avitelmessus—These little crabs scuttle along on four pairs of legs. Watch out, those pincers can nip!

Scaphites—See if you can spot these ammonites peeking out of their shells.

TIDAL POOLS

Best to stick to the tidal pools. It may not be as spectacular, but smaller sea life is taking on all kinds of strange shapes and forms.

Spondylus—These clamlike shellfish are still found in warm seas today.

FIELD GUIDE:
FOLLOW THE HERD

The Cretaceous provides a whole new range of plants for herbivores to feast on. And now there's a lot more of them coming to the table!

Lambeosaurus

LEFT TURN!

Maiasaura

Parasaurolophus

Safety in numbers

Sauropods are now far outnumbered by smaller herbivores, especially the hadrosaurs, or duck-billed dinosaurs. Hanging out in herds gives these guys protection against predators. And because they all eat different plants, they don't compete for food.

Edmontosaurus

Beyond the bill

KEEP UP BACK THERE!

An Edmontosaurus may have as many as 1,600 teeth!

The duck-billed dinosaurs are named for their broad mouths. Although they have no front teeth, they can still grasp and pull off leaves with their strong lips. At the back of their mouths are hundreds of tiny, leaf-shaped teeth for shredding plants before swallowing.

STAND BACK! MUST BE RUSH HOUR!

Snout covered in tough, leathery skin

Mass transit

With the weather changing from season to season, plants grow in different places throughout the year. So herds of hadrosaurs and other plant eaters are traveling longer distances to gather food.

A HEADS-UP

Clearly, if you really want to be fashionable in the Cretaceous, you need some eye-catching headgear. Can you look the part?

Olorotitan

STANDING OUT

With their impressive crests, horns, lumps, and bumps, many of the hadrosaurs really stand out from the crowd.

Corythosaurus

Stygimoloch

Pachycephalosaurus

HARD HATS

Another group of herbivores, the pachycephalosaurs, have dome-shaped heads fringed by knobs, studs, and spikes. Although these dashing domes are mainly for display, pachycephalosaurs may also use their hard hats to head-butt rivals or predators. Can you find out?

Lambeosaurus

Parasaurolophus

WHAT A HOOT!

Horns and crests help hadrosaurs communicate. By blowing air through hollow tubes inside these protrusions, hadrosaurs make honking or hooting sounds, and the different shapes of horns give each species a different sound. Can you figure out what they are saying?

HONK?
(HEY, JEFF. HOW'S IT GOING?)

TOOT!
(CAN'T COMPLAIN, LARRY!)

FIELD GUIDE:

THE ARMORED DIVISION

Big, heavy herbivores that can't move quickly need stout defenses against fast-moving predators. Armor, shields, and an array of weapons provide maximum protection.

AS I WAS SAYING . . .

Tough stuff

Edmontonia—Sharp shoulder spikes keep predators at bay and can be used to attack, too. Bony plates and spikes protect the back and tail.

These herbivores, known as ankylosaurs, might not be bulletproof, but they sure are thick-skinned! Their impressive body armor provides a last line of defense against slashing claws, tearing talons, and fearsome fangs.

HEAD-ON

The best bet for ceratopsians— the great, lumbering rhino-like herbivores of the Cretaceous— is to meet their attackers head-on. While their high, bony frills shield their necks and backs, they thrust forward with their deadly horns, even charging at a predator before it makes its first move. Their distinctive arrangements of frill and horns will help you get to know them.

SPOT THE ODD ONE OUT!

YEAH, HE'S SO CUTE!

Centrosaurus—Its single horn is its main weapon. The small ones at the top of the frill and around the edge are more for show.

Triceratops—This is one of the biggest and certainly the most famous ceratopsian. Its horns may be up to 28 in. (70 cm) long.

BIFF!

CLUBS WIN

Ankylosaurus and *Euoplocephalus* both have a heavy club at the end of their tail. Swung hard at an attacker, it can be a real knockout!

URGH! I REALLY NEED TO WORK OUT MORE!

LOW SLUNG

The underparts of ankylosaurs are unprotected. But because they are so low to the ground, it's hard for even the biggest predator to turn them over.

Ankylosaurus–Triangular horns jut out from the skull. Hundreds of armor-like plates cover the head, back, and flanks.

Euoplocephalus–Ridged oval plates cover most of the body, and there are spikes on the shoulders and cheeks. Even the eyes are protected by stiff plates.

Chasmosaurus–Above its three large horns, inside the skin, are two wide openings, or "chasms." Colors and patterns decorate the skin.

DON'T CALL ME CUTE! I HATE THAT!

Protoceratops–This little guy has no horns and only a small frill, but its powerful beak conceals two pairs of pointed teeth.

Einiosaurus–This guy's oddly angled horns don't seem terribly practical! But they are handy for both defense and display.

Titanoceratops–This humungous herbivore has three large forward-facing spikes and two cheek horns.

I'VE GOT THE BIGGEST SKULL OF ANY LAND ANIMAL EVER.

FIELD GUIDE:
ULTIMATE THREATS

In the Late Cretaceous, every step you take could be your last. You can't make a move without the utmost care. And you need to be constantly on your guard, paying attention to every rustle, roar, and rumble. For this is the time of some of the most savage killers that ever lived.

Weighing in

Sensing some stealthy footsteps? You could be getting stalked by a giant theropod carnivore. Every continent has these monstrous killers, the ultimate killing machines of their age. So how do these heavyweights match up?

Tyrannosaurus's bite is so strong that it could chomp through a car!

GRRR!

HEY! STOP SHOWING OFF. YOU'D BETTER SAVE YOUR STRENGTH FOR ME!

TYRANNOSAURUS
Not called "the king" for nothing. This North American crowd-pleaser has a solid record of steady slaughter.

Size: 39 ft. (12 m)
Weight: 7.5 tons (6.8 tonnes)
Strengths: Unrivaled biting power, terrifying reputation
Weaknesses: Tiny arms, not the fastest on its feet

CARCHARODONTOSAURUS
The African champion is always well prepared: check out the massive, well-toned muscles, streamlined head, and killer smile!

Size: 44 ft. (13.5 m)
Weight: 7.7 tons (7 tonnes)
Strengths: Powerful build, long serrated teeth—like those of a great white shark
Weaknesses: Lacks popular support, but that's not likely to be a major disadvantage here

GIGANOTOSAURUS

If looks could kill, this temperamental South American would slay them all: powerful body, bristling with bony horns and ridges, and a terrifying stare.

Size: 43 ft. (13 m)
Weight: 7.7 tons (7 tonnes)
Strengths: Bony lumps and horns on the head and body provide extra protection
Weaknesses: Weak arms; tends to rely on backup, so could struggle a little in a one-on-one

TARBOSAURUS

Unrivaled on its home turf in Asia, *Tarbosaurus* displays most of the qualities of its relative, *Tyrannosaurus*. Could be the, uh, dark horse of the competition.

Size: 35 ft. (11 m)
Weight: 6.8 tons (6.2 tonnes)
Strengths: More teeth than its famous cousin and a more streamlined body
Weaknesses: The arms, of course, and it's lighter than most of its rivals

STAYING SAFE

- Everywhere you go, find a safe haven to which you can beat a hasty retreat. A high tree with thick foliage is a good choice.
- Learn to spot signs of danger, such as freshly made theropod tracks and droppings.
- Carry stones and sharpened sticks to ward off attackers.
- Keep your fingers crossed that you look too weird to eat.

TIME'S UP!

Living with ever-present danger is exhausting. What's more, the skies are darkening, and it's getting harder to breathe. And what's that glowing light in the sky? It was great to be around for the start of the age of the dinosaurs, but you really don't want to be here at the end. The party is over: time to head home!

Broome X

Richmond X X Hughenden

X Winton

X Lark Quarry

Roma X

BRISBANE •

AUSTRALIA

They've vanished without a trace, but they made a lasting impression. See page 137.

Can you help this guy find his feet? Turn to page 130.

How did this little plant-eater keep predators in the dark? Find out on page 139.

SYDNEY •

MELBOURNE

They're between some rocks and a very hard place. See page 138.

Dinosaur Cove

Inverloch X

X

Antarctic Peninsula X

ANTARCTICA

Mount Kirkpatrick X

It looks small here, but Antarctica is almost twice the size of Australia!

Sno' joke hunting in Antarctica, even if the locals are warm and friendly. See page 140.

What do the patterns reveal? See page 136.

DIGGING DOWN UNDER

Following a tip from a local expert, you've traveled far into the Australian desert to an isolated rocky outcrop. After scaling its flank, you're walking across a wide, sloping slab when you spy what you were seeking: a dinosaur footprint, probably 100 million years old! The trackway continues upward, vanishing at times beneath sand and shrubs, then reappearing. Enthralled by your discovery, eyes glued to the ground, you continue upward—unaware of the looming cliff edge. It's only as your foot steps out over the void that your companion's hand reaches out—to haul you back from a fateful plunge to the desert far below.

Hawke's Bay

NEW ZEALAND

Imagine finding one of these in your main street! See page 134.

Can you tell it's a tail? Joan could. Learn more on page 131.

HUNTER'S QUEST

Though they were once joined, the world's most southerly landmasses (Australia, New Zealand, and Antarctica) are now separated by vast expanses of wind-whipped ocean. Not many fossils have been found here. But that's partly because these sparsely populated lands don't have as many dinosaur hunters as other continents. Can you help reveal more about dinos "down under?"

Few and far between

Australia has been the region's main fossil source, and it's fairly easy to reach and travel around. But most of the land is flat. There are few high mountains and deeply eroded canyons where fossils are exposed—just a few small islands of Mesozoic surface rocks dotted around vast expanses of blisteringly hot, virtually empty desert.

> Australia is as big as the mainland United States, but has only one person for every 15 in the USA.

GHOSTS OF GONDWANA

Dinosaur life in these realms remains something of a mystery. There have been no Triassic finds at all, and the Jurassic record consists of only a few partial skeletons and small scraps of bone. So there's plenty for you to do!

> THE REST OF ME IS OUT THERE SOMEWHERE!

Australia, New Zealand, and Antarctica were all once part of the southern continent of Gondwana, which included South America, Africa, and India. By the Early Cretaceous, 120 million years ago, Australia and Antarctica were a long way from anywhere else, and New Zealand was under ocean.

This small meat-eater from Australia, named Ozraptor, is known only from one small piece of leg bone.

ONE-OFFS

If you came across the object at right, what would you think it was? A fossilized giant insect? A Maori carving? A backscratcher? Found by amateur fossil hunter, Joan Wiffen at Hawke's Bay, New Zealand, in 1975, it turned out to be a theropod tailbone. That made it the country's first ever dinosaur fossil.

Joan Wiffen

New Zealand's spectacular marine fossils include giant ammonites.

Since then, though, only a few others have been found (mainly by Joan Wiffen): one Jurassic claw bone and a few Cretaceous bones and teeth. That's mainly because most of New Zealand lay under sea during the Mesozoic. Which makes it a top spot for marine fossils!

Out of reach

It's not surprising that hardly any dinosaur fossils have been dug up in Antarctica. For a start, it's the coldest and windiest place on Earth. And just getting there is a major expedition—it usually involves a long boat trip from Australia or South America, weaving through colossal icebergs and pack ice as you near this virtually unpopulated land. What's more, 98 percent of it is covered by ice. Now there's a challenge for you!

SOME OF THAT ICE IS 3 MI. (5 KM) DEEP!

WOW! I DIDN'T KNOW THAT!

JEWELS IN THE DUST

Meager they might be, but from the start, Australia's dinosaur remains have included important and highly unusual finds. Imagine, for example, digging up a dinosaur bone that has turned into a gemstone—treasure of two types in one!

Opalized tooth

THE WAY AHEAD

It was a fossilized finger that first pointed the way for Australian dinosaur hunters, in 1903. Geologist, William Ferguson was surveying the southeast coast near Inverloch in Victoria, when he spotted a shiny 2 in. (5 cm) claw poking out of a rock. He had to send it to London, England to have his suspicions confirmed: that it was Australia's first dinosaur fossil.

THIS WAY, PLEASE!

Rhoetosaurus is one of the oldest sauropod specimens in the world.

I'M HIGHLY CULTIVATED!

BUMPER CROP

A puzzled farmer found mysterious blackened bones on his property near Roma in southern Queensland, in 1924. He sent samples to paleontologist, Heber Longman at the Queensland Museum in Brisbane, who then traveled to the site and dug up another 800 lb. (400 kg) of fossils. He identified them as parts of a Mid-Jurassic sauropod, and named the species *Rhoetosaurus*, after Rhoetos, a giant in Greek mythology.

IT'S ALL GREEK TO ME!

Opalized thigh bone of small plant-eater, *Fulgurotherium*

Real gems

> **IF YOU'VE GOT IT, FLAUNT IT!**

Many opalized fossils have been found at the town of Lightning Ridge in New South Wales, Australia.

Jewels in the shape of dinosaur bones and teeth—that's what you get when fossils become opalized. Opal is a precious stone that forms underground over millions of years when a mixture of water and a mineral called silica solidifies inside rock. If, instead, the mixture fills a hole formed by a bone, tooth, shell, or other body part—presto!—a stunningly colorful, doubly precious fossil.

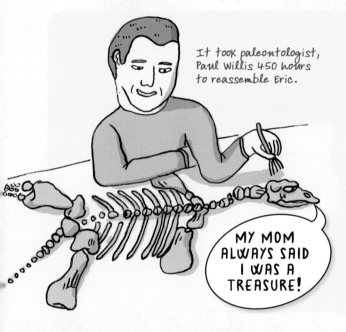

It took paleontologist, Paul Willis 450 hours to reassemble Eric.

> **MY MOM ALWAYS SAID I WAS A TREASURE!**

DIG DEEPER

· · · · · · · · · · · · · · · · · · · ·

AUSTRALIAN MUSEUM, SYDNEY

In 1987 a miner digging for opals at Coober Pedy in South Australia hit paydirt—an entire opalized skeleton of an Early Cretaceous pliosaur. When in 1993 the owner of this treasure decided to sell it to an overseas collector, schoolchildren all over Australia helped raise money to buy it for the nation. Now the skeleton, known to his many pals as Eric, is on display at Sydney's Australian Museum, alongside a fantastic collection of other local dinosaur fossils.

Mini Mi

Many fossils of the armored-tank-like dinosaurs known as ankylosaurs have been dug up in the Northern Hemisphere, but very few in the Southern Hemisphere. By far the most complete is *Minmi*, a pint-sized ankylosaur found in 1964, near Roma, Queensland.

Minmi had a very small brain. Was it just young, stupid—or both?!

Armor plates and spikes protect the upper body.

THE FOSSIL TRIANGLE

It's a hot spot in more ways than one. The district around the outback towns of Richmond, Hughenden, and Winton in Queensland, Australia, consists of great stretches of sweltering, Sun-baked scrub, where summers are scorching. But it's also been the source of many of Australia's major dinosaur finds, which has earned it the name of the Fossil Triangle.

Large nostrils and a bony lump on snout—possibly an inflatable sac used to make loud calls

Strong teeth for slicing through tough plants

You might need to look twice on the main street of Hughenden. A fiberglass replica of *Muttaburrasaurus*, known locally as "Mutt," looms over passing cars and pedestrians.

A total Mutt

In 1963 a rockpile in a sheep yard near the small settlement of Muttaburra was found to be a cluster of colossal dinosaur bones. A call went out to local farmers to bring in any similar fossils they had on their land. Eventually 60 percent of a skeleton was assembled and the species was named *Muttaburrasaurus*.

One *Muttaburrasaurus* skull, found by a teenager called Robert Walker, was used by his family as a doorstop for years.

Scourge of the seas

One hundred million years ago, much of this region was flooded by sea. *Kronosaurus*, a huge 30 ft. (9 m) pliosaur, was the scourge of these waters, feasting on huge fish and savaging other marine reptiles. There are fossils and a life-size model at the Kronosaurus Korner museum in Richmond.

YUM, SHOULD BE A HAPPY SNAP!

Hidden danger

IT'S A BUMPY ROAD!

Riding his motorbike across his sheep farm in 1999, farmer Dave Elliott almost crashed into what looked like a big boulder hidden in long grass. It proved to be the massive thigh bone of a sauropod that may have been up to 69 ft. (21 m) long—still the biggest dinosaur ever discovered in Australia. A few other bone fragments have been found, but not enough to identify the species. So the fossil is still known simply as "Elliott."

Poet's corner

In 2009 a trove of dinosaurs was discovered on a remote sheep and cattle farm, Elderslie Station. All three were given nicknames relating to one of Australia's most famous poets, Andrew "Banjo" Paterson, composer of the song, "Waltzing Matilda," who once worked on the station.

Wintonotitan, or "Clancy" (after a poem by Paterson), was an even bigger sauropod.

Armored plates on back

Australovenator, or "Banjo" for short, was a small, speedy predator. It was compared to a cheetah by its finders.

Diamantinasaurus, nicknamed "Matilda," was a chunky sauropod up to 52 ft. (16 m) long.

DIG DEEPER

AUSTRALIAN AGE OF DINOSAURS MUSEUM

You can find out more about all these dinosaurs, and see their fossils, at this museum southeast of Winton. Not only that, you can help prepare finds, get advice on local fossil sites, and sign up for regular digs.

A MOMENT IN TIME?

At Lark Quarry near Winton in Queensland, Australia, you'll find one of the world's most remarkable sets of dinosaur footprints. Its multiple criss-crossing tracks conjure up an intriguing Cretaceous scene. But what exactly was going on here?

Feet first

First studied by paleontologists in 1971, the prints at Lark Quarry lay on a rock slab in a shallow valley. After surrounding rock and rubble was cleared, a total of more than 3,000 footprints were revealed! The prints are now protected inside a modern visitor center.

How to make fossilized footprints

1 Find some mud with clay mixed into it. Make a series of deep prints. Leave to bake in Sun.

2 Once hard, cover with a thick layer of sand.

3 Leave to harden for, oh, 70 million years.

4 Uncover and enjoy!

WAY OF THE GIANTS

Dinosaur footprints on the seashore near Broome, on the northwest coast of Australia, are among the biggest ever found. First spotted in the 1930s by a group of Girl Scouts, the prints were later found to extend for 50 mi. (80 km) along the coast. The largest were more than 3 ft. (1 m) in diameter, which meant they belonged to dinosaurs bigger than any discovered so far!

Sadly fossil hunters stole several of the footprints—including the world's only stegosaur print!

Cast of hundreds

Initially, it appeared that most of the prints at Lark Quarry belonged to around 180 dinosaurs of two small species: a chicken-size carnivore called *Skartopus* and a slightly bigger herbivore, *Wintonopus*. These guys appeared to be traveling together. A set of other, much bigger tracks was thought to be those of a lone *Tyrannosauropus*, a 30 ft. (10 m) meat-eater.

FLIGHT FOR LIFE?

The smaller dinosaurs were moving fast. Were they running for their lives, past and away from an attacking predator? Was this the first ever fossil record of a dinosaur stampede?

WHEN DO I COME IN?

Tyrannosauropus

Muttaburrasaurus

Wintonopus

YOU DON'T, I'M UP NEXT.

NOW, YOU RUN THAT WAY.

Skartopus

HANG ON, WHO'S CHASING WHO?

PAWS FOR THOUGHT

Maybe. But recently doubts have been cast on this idea. It seems that the small prints were made over several days, that there may have been only one species of small dinosaur, and that the large dinosaur was not *Tyrannosauropus* but *Muttaburrasaurus*, a herbivore. Can you make sense of it?

LAND OF THE LONG NIGHT

With its wild winds, huge tides, and treacherous cliffs, Dinosaur Cove in southeastern Australia will really test your mettle. And about 100 million years ago, it was a trying place for dinosaurs, too.

Wild shore

THREE WEEKS AND THAT'S ALL WE'VE MANAGED?!

Dinosaur Cove has been one of Australia's most productive fossil sites. Yet working here is hugely challenging. For a start, it's a long hike from the nearest road to this remote headland. The cliffs are battered by waves, rain and howling winds, and the rocks are so hard you need drills or even explosives to get at the fossils.

Coping with winter

In the Early Cretaceous, Australia was far south of its current location, partly inside the Antarctic Circle. Antarctica wasn't as cold as it is today, and thick forests covered much of the land, but it was still pretty chilly. And, as now, the winter included a three-month period of near-total darkness. So how did dinosaurs deal with this?

Small herbivores like Leaellynasaura may have hibernated for part of the time in burrows, surviving on energy stored in their body fat, as many polar animals do today.

ZZZZZZZ

THAT'S OUR GIRL!

WHICH ONE?

Proud parents

The site was first explored in the 1970s, but the most important excavations began in 1984 and were carried out by paleontologists, Tom Rich and Patricia Vickers-Rich—over a ten-year period! After all that hard work, it was only fair that they got to name a couple of species—*Timimus* and *Leaellynasaura*—after their kids, Tim and Leaellyn.

Leaellyn Rich   *Leaellynasaura*

BRAND NAMES

Dinosaur hunters often need a lot of help. One way to thank people who have helped you out is to name a dinosaur after them. The Riches called one dinosaur, *Atlascopcosaurus*, after the company that provided their drills, Atlas Copco. And when they later dug at another site, further east along the coast near Inverloch, they named another dinosaur *Qantassaurus*, after the Australian airline, Qantas, which helped with travel.

Qantassaurus

Atlascopcosaurus

ENTOMBED IN ICE

Could this be the ultimate challenge? To travel to the end of the earth, tough it out in subfreezing weather and hurricane-force winds, and tunnel through snow, ice, and frozen soil to reach rare, undiscovered fossils? Finding and naming a new species could be your greatest reward.

YOU'RE GOING THE WRONG WAY. THERE ARE NO FISH UP THERE!

Snow go

Going to Antarctica by ship is a good idea, because it takes a boatload of equipment to tackle this task. Load up on drills, ice picks, food supplies, maps, and emergency equipment. Don't forget you'll need layers of super-warm clothing—and, ideally, your own on-snow transport!

Wind speeds along the coast of Antarctica can reach up to 185 mph (300km/h)!

Easy does it

The only part of Antarctica that remains free of ice and snow for long is the Antarctic Peninsula, a long, narrow spit of land that reaches up toward South America. Not surprisingly, it's where the first Antarctic dinosaur remains were discovered, in 1986 (parts of a small ankylosaur, *Antarctopelta*), and it's still the best place to start.

YOU'VE GOT TO BE THICK-SKINNED TO LIVE HERE!

Antarctopelta

From on high

Once you've acclimated, you might want to venture further into the continent. Look for exposed rocks. In 1992 on Mount Kirkpatrick in the Transantarctic Mountains, dinosaur hunters found a hoard of 60 bones. They included two new Early Jurassic species, *Cryolophosaurus* and *Glacialisaurus*.

FROZEN HERBIVORE

Known only from fragments, *Glacialisaurus* was a sauropod that may have been related to China's *Lufengosaurus* (see page 107). Its name comes from the Latin *glacialis*, meaning "frozen."

> I'VE TOLD YOU: CHEW BEFORE YOU SWALLOW!

The remains of one *Cryolophosaurus* suggest it choked to death trying to eat another dino!

JUST DANDY!

Perhaps the most exciting find yet from Antarctica, *Cryolophosaurus* was a fierce Jurassic predator with a distinctive head crest. The crest resembled the hair of Elvis Presley, which led to the dinosaur being referred to as "Elvisaurus!"

WAITING TO BE FOUND

To survive, a large predator like *Cryolophosaurus* must have had plenty of meat to feast on. That means there must have been many other dinosaurs living here, and that far more fossils are entombed beneath the Antarctic ice. So, get digging!

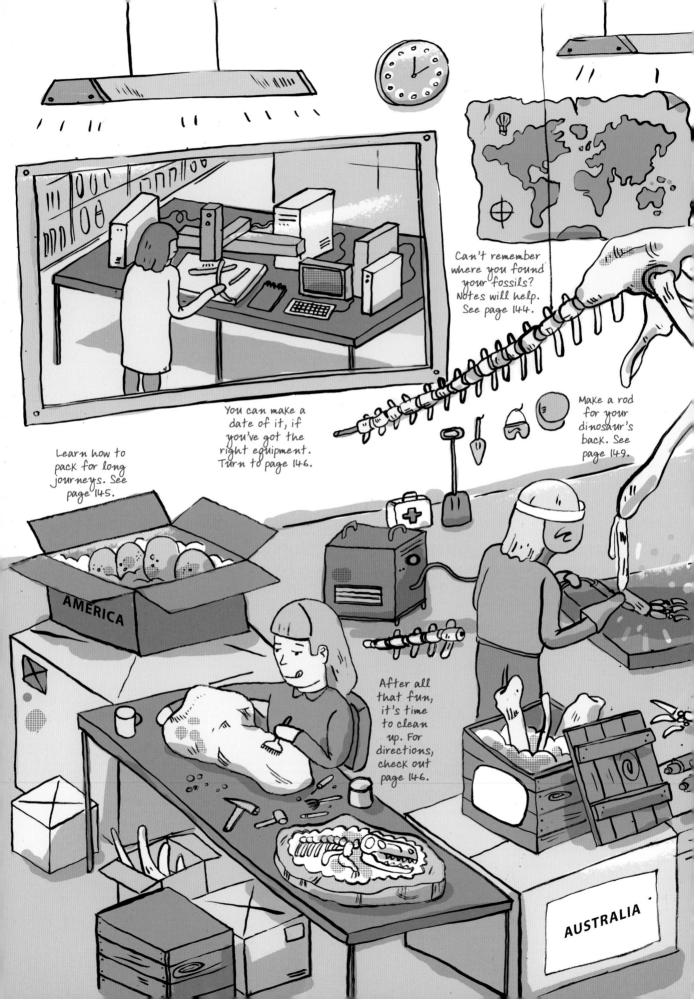

PIECING IT TOGETHER

If any pieces of the puzzle are missing— just make them! Find out how on page 149.

Your travels are over. But the real work has just begun. Poring through your treasure trove, you single out an intriguing set of fossils. Closer examination and consultations with experts suggest they're from an entirely new species. You and your team swing into action. Bones are matched up. A skeleton is assembled. You sketch how it could have looked, imagine its skin and coloring. Finally, you create a lifelike computer animation, and there it is, walking once more, brought back to life after 120 million years— your very own dinosaur.

By the time you've finished, it'll be a virtual reality. See page 151.

Skulls give you a head start. See page 147.

EUROPE

GOOD TO GO

So, you've found a fossil? Great. But, whoa, don't just yank it out! You have to work carefully to keep your find as intact as possible, and take time to gather every shred of information that might help you identify it. Be patient. After all, it's been there millions of years—it deserves a gentle awakening!

Mark the spot

Clear any loose debris around the fossil. Then, reach for your notepad and pencil, rather than your hammer and chisel. Note where you have found the fossil: at what time, at what location, in what kind of rock? Look for other fossils nearby.

I THINK THAT'S ITS BEST SIDE!

Take photos of the site.

Draw a map of the fossil's position.

Collect rock samples—these could help you date your find.

FINDERS KEEPERS?

It's seldom true. In fact, by taking a fossil home, you could be committing a crime. In many countries there are strict rules about removing fossils from public or private land. If you are unsure, ask at a local museum or government office—before you start swinging that hammer!

Chip away

Is the fossil embedded in rock? How you extract it depends on the type of rock. With hard stone, you might need to use drills or even explosives. But with softer sedimentary rock, you can first, chip away at the surrounding material with a pick. Then, use a hammer and chisel to break off smaller pieces.

Work carefully around the edges of the fossil.

A brush will come in handy for removing loose dirt.

Once you've cleared the surface, you may have to dig under the fossil to get it out of the ground.

Padded parcel

Transporting fossils is a tricky business. Even though they are rock hard, they can be very fragile. Wrap smaller specimens in tissue paper or bubble wrap and pack them in sturdy boxes. To protect larger fossils, you'll need to make a plaster cast:

❶ First, cover the fossil in paper towels, wet newspaper, or aluminum foil.

❷ Next, mix up some plaster and dip strips of sackcloth in the plaster.

❸ Wrap the fossil in several layers of the cloth. Leave to harden.

THEROPOD BONE, 9/30/13
FOSSIL VALLEY, USA
–> DINO HUNTER HQ

❹ Label with identification details—name, date, and place of find, and destination.

This should provide protection from knocks and sudden bumps. Fingers crossed!

GLAD WE'RE ON THE LAST LEG!

Shipping out

If your fossil is big, let's hope you don't have to carry it far! You may need several hands to haul it to the nearest road or vehicle. Fossils found overseas may have to be sent home in planes or boats, and so will need extra protection.

SCARY!

OUT OF YOUR HANDS

You can take all the care you like, but sometimes things are beyond your control. Dinosaur hunter, Charles Sternberg pioneered the technique of wrapping fossils in plaster prior to shipping. In 1916 he had 22 crates of fossils transported to London aboard the ship SS *Mount Temple*. But the First World War was in full swing and a German ship sank the *Mount Temple*. Today, the fossils lie 14,440 ft. (4,375 m) below the surface of the Atlantic Ocean.

LOOKING FOR CLUES

Once your fossils are safely back home, you'd better roll up your sleeves and get busy. First, you'll need to clean and preserve the fossils. Then, you start the painstaking business of working out exactly what you have found!

How to prepare a fossil

1 Scrape away the last bits of rock using your drills and chisels. You can even use small picks like the ones your dentist uses on your teeth.

THIS WON'T HURT A BIT . . .

Be careful! It's better to leave some rock on the fossil rather than risk damaging it.

2 For more stubborn attachments, you can use a tool called an air scribe, which blasts a jet of air at the stone. Or, you may have to use chemicals, such as acids to dissolve really strong rock.

3 Finally, to keep your fossil strong, paint it with consolidant, a glue-like substance that sets hard and protects the surface.

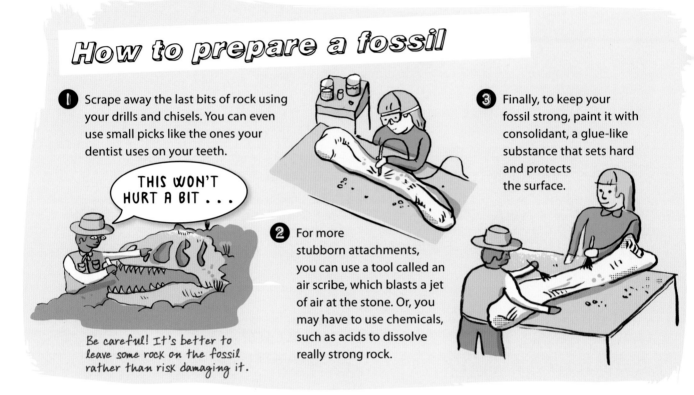

100 mya

150 mya

200 mya

250 mya

THE DATING GAME

Sandstone

If you have taken careful note of the age of the rocks at the site where you made your find, or know the ages of other fossils found there, that will give you an idea of your fossil's age.

If you don't, you may need some high-tech help to date your find. Scientists use various techniques to work out the age of rocks, usually based

Granite

on measuring the rate of decay of radioactive substances in the rocks over millions of years. Hope you brought back those rock samples!

Basalt   *Volcanic rocks like basalt are best for dating.*

Positive ID

Dinosaur hunters seldom find complete skeletons. So you will probably have to identify your find from only a few bones.

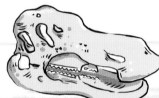

HMM, NOT QUITE RIGHT!

FAMILY TRAITS

Work out what other dinosaurs were around in the area your fossil comes from. Locate fossils or models of those dinosaurs and compare them with yours. Are there any similarities?

HEAD START

If one of your bones is a skull, it will make identifying the dinosaur much easier, as most skulls have features that are particular to a group or species.

Massive skulls with long, curved, pointed teeth are usually from large carnivores.

Duck-shaped bills usually belong to hadrosaurs.

A combination of horns and frill are a dead giveaway for a ceratopsian like Triceratops.

STANDING OUT

If you don't have a skull, identification is trickier but there are still some handy clues in many bones.

The position of the pubis bone in the pelvis will tell you if a dinosaur was bird-hipped or lizard-hipped (skip back to page 11 if you can't remember what that's about!).

Saurischian or lizard-hipped: All the meat-eaters, plus plant-eating sauropods and prosauropods

Ornithischian or bird-hipped: All other plant-eaters

Small arm bones found with much bigger leg bones could belong to a theropod, such as *Tyrannosaurus*. Theropods walked on two legs, but some had tiny, weak arms.

A massive leg bone as tall as you is likely to be from a sauropod, like *Diplodocus*. A bone of that size tells you that the dinosaur was huge!

SHAPING UP

Now that you're getting to know your dinosaur, you'll want to give it a name. You might also like to get a clearer picture of how it looked—by putting it back together!

What's in a name?

You might decide to call your dinosaur Dave or Dina, but if you are a proper paleontologist, you have to give it a scientific name, using Latin or Greek terms. Scientific names have two elements: the group or genus name and the species name. For example, *Yutyrannus huali* is so far the only species of the *Yutyrannus* genus, a branch of the Tyrannosaur family from China. If you found a new *Yutyrannus*, you could add a species name of your choice: *Yutyrannus dinosaurhunterus*? And if you find a new genus, you get to choose the whole name—any ideas?

> YES, I AM RATHER LOVELY!

Yutyrannus means "feathered tyrant," and *huali* means "beautiful."

SHEEP'S CLOTHING?

One of the oddest choices of name for a dinosaur was for a small theropod discovered in 1993 by 14-year-old fossil hunter Wes Linster, in Montana, USA. Because the dinosaur was small and young, it was named *Bambiraptor*, after the Walt Disney character. This was no kid-friendly creature, however, but a fierce carnivore with razor-sharp teeth and huge hooked talons that probably ate cute baby mammals for breakfast!

You can use some of these Latin and Greek terms to help you make up new genus names:

PREFIX (for start of word)	SUFFIX (for end of word)
Dino — *Terrible*	-saurus — *lizard*
Di — *Two*	-gnathus — *jaw*
Tri — *Three*	-nychus — *claw*
Micro — *Small*	-venator — *hunter*
Megalo — *Large*	
Teratos — *Monster*	-mimus — *imitator*
Stegos — *Plated*	-raptor — *thief*
Saltus — *Jumping*	-ceratops — *horned face*

> *Brontosaurus* used to be a famous dinosaur. But then, paleontologists realized it was actually the same as *Apatosaurus*. And because *Apatosaurus* had been named first, it was bye-bye *Brontosaurus*!

Filling in the gaps

Even if you have only a few bones from an identified dinosaur, you can work out what the rest looked like by comparing your find with other, more complete fossils of the same species or group. Then, you can make models of the missing bones and even construct an entire skeleton.

LOOKING GOOD!

How to build a skeleton

1 Make molds of missing bones by painting latex or rubber onto fossils or other copies of bones.

2 Fill mold with plaster or plastic resin to make a new cast.

3 When cast is hard, remove mold. Paint cast to look like fossil.

4 Build a frame out of metal rods. Bend into desired shape. Do you want your dinosaur to be standing, running—hopping (maybe not)? Attach fossils or casts to rods in correct order.

Allow plenty of time. Most vertebrate skeletons have more than 200 separate bones!

Often real bones are replaced by casts on skeletons. The casts are stronger and much lighter, and they can be replaced if damaged.

In the best mounts, the framework is hardly visible and the pose looks natural and correct.

IT'S GREAT TO BE BACK ON TWO FEET— EVEN IF THEY'RE NOT MINE!

BACK TO LIFE

A skeleton shows you the size and general shape of your dinosaur. But it doesn't show you what it really looked like—its body features and skin color, how it moved and sounded, and so on. But paleontologists can work much of this out by studying fossils and modern, living creatures. And artists can now produce astonishingly lifelike recreations of dinosaurs—as models, on paper, and computer and movie screens.

Same insides

Only very rarely are traces of organs found in dinosaur fossils. But it seems likely that they would have had the same or similar organs to other creatures, especially modern relatives, such as birds and crocodiles.

HEY, I THINK I MIGHT BE A DINOSAUR!

WAIT TILL I SHOW YOU MY MOVES!

Building muscle

Marks on bones show where muscles were attached. Based on studies of other creatures, palaeontologists can work out how the muscles were positioned and connected. The size of the bones indicates roughly how big they were.

TRY STEALING MY EGGS NOW!

A NEW BREED?

In the book and movie series, *Jurassic Park*, scientists clone dinosaurs using fossilised dinosaur DNA (a substance in all creatures that contains instructions for building that life form). Is that possible? Well, it's highly unlikely anyone will find dinosaur DNA, as DNA starts breaking down after hundreds of years and is untraceable after a mere 6.8 million years. But there might be another way . . .

Horner aims to create what he calls "chickenosaurus."

US paleontologist Jack Horner (see page 62) is trying to modify the DNA of chickens (modern relatives of dinosaurs) so that they evolve backward, and develop some dinosaur characteristics, such as teeth, long tails, and arms.

MMM, COZY!

True colors

No fossil preserves the colors of dinosaur skin. So all images of dinosaur skin are guesswork. Some experts think all dinosaurs would have had dull, earthy colors for camouflage. But others believe that some would have had bright colors and patterns—as many birds do—to attract mates. Your guess is as good as anyone's!

YEAH, I LIKE THAT. COOL!

On the surface

Impressions found on some fossils provide a guide to skin patterns and textures. It was previously assumed that all dinosaurs were scaly, like most modern reptiles. But we now know many had feathers—even some of the bigger ones!

IMAGINE MEETING THAT!

HIGHLY ANIMATED

Since the early 1800s, artists have worked with paleontologists to recreate dinosaurs in drawings, paintings, and sculpture. And today, using computer graphics software, artists can create moving, breathing, growling representations that are frighteningly real!

The real thing?

AARGH! LET'S GET OUT OF HERE!

Sophisticated robot, or animatronic, versions can also be created. These are so lifelike you'd swear you'd taken a trip back in time!

INDEX

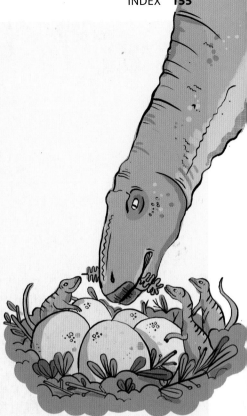

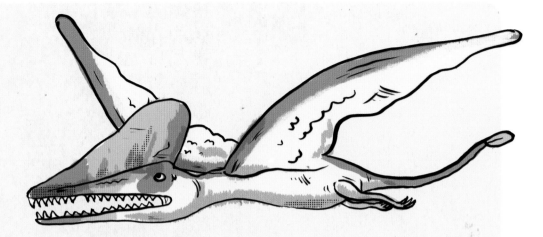

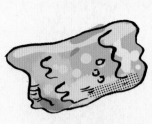
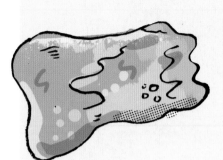

1st Edition
Published September 2013

WELDONOWEN

Conceived by Weldon Owen in partnership with Lonely Planet
Produced by Weldon Owen
An imprint of Red Lemon Press Limited
Northburgh House, 10 Northburgh Street, London EC1V 0AT, UK
Copyright © 2013 Weldon Owen Limited

www.redlemonpress.com
Red Lemon Press Limited is part of the Bonnier Publishing Group
www.bonnierpublishing.com

Author and Project Manager Scott Forbes, Solas Text & Design
Designer Cathy Campbell, Solas Text & Design
Illustrator © James Gulliver Hancock/The Jacky Winter Group
Consultant Dr. Paul Willis, Director, RiAus (riaus.org.au)
Project Editor Ariana Klepac

Published by
Lonely Planet Publications Pty Ltd ABN 36 005 607 983
90 Maribyrnong St, Footscray, Victoria 3011, Australia

ISBN 978-1-7432-1908-9

Printed and bound in China by 1010 Printing Int Ltd
10 9 8 7 6 5 4 3 2 1

The author and illustrator would like to dedicate this book, respectively, to Ruari and Quinn, budding dinosaur hunters.

Also available in the series

LONELY PLANET OFFICES

Australia Head Office
Locked Bag 1, Footscray, Victoria 3011
phone 03 8379 8000
fax 03 8379 8111

USA
150 Linden St., Oakland, CA 94607
phone 510-250-6400
toll free 800-275-8555
fax 510-893-8572

UK
Media Centre, 201 Wood Lane,
London W12 7TQ
phone 020 8433 1333
fax 020 8702 0112

lonelyplanet.com/contact